Published in Santa Rosa Beach, Florida by My Honest Answers
www.myhonestanswers.com

Cover and Interior Design by Laura Burton Design
www.lauraburtondesign.com

ISBN 978-0-9791663-0-3

Printed in the United States of America

God, Me
MY IN-LAW &

MOTHERS AND
DAUGHTERS-IN-LAW
TELL IT
LIKE IT IS

AUTHORS PAM EASON, JANE JONES, AND JANE MILLS

Dedication

*T*o all those mothers and daughters-in-law who are striving to strengthen their challenging but God-ordained relationship for the purpose of honoring God.

Acknowledgments

Our deep thanks to all the mothers and daughters-in-law who expressed a sincere desire to improve their relationship, encouraged us in this monumental task, contributed their intimate stories, and participated in the electronic survey that added so much validity to our endeavor. Thanks to those who reviewed our chapters, made suggestions, helped us with changes, and to those who were patient enough to help compile the survey data. Our hearty thanks to Mike Eason who spent days setting up, monitoring, and organizing our data collection process.

The survey data, collected in 2006, needs a bit of explanation. Sixty-five mothers and daughters-in-law, ages 23 to 77, contributed to the data. It's important to note ALL surveys used were from in-laws who said they were followers of Jesus Christ. Many women who took the survey commented that the questions helped them reflect on their own in-law relationship and encouraged them to consider their participation in this relationship from God's perspective.

To review the types of questions on the survey or to take the in-law survey yourself, go to www.myhonestanswers.com on the web.

Table of Contents

Forward by Lynne Ballard 8

Introduction 10

Chapter 1 – Wise Whitney 14

Chapter 2 – Patient Patty 22

Chapter 3 – Selfish Sally 32

Chapter 4 – Overly-Sensitive Olivia 40

Chapter 5 – Unforgiving Janice 48

Chapter 6 – Complaining Carol 58

Chapter 7 – Aspiring Allison 66

Chapter 8 – Burdensome Britney 74

Chapter 9 – Intolerant Tess 82

Chapter 10 – Jealous Judy 90

Chapter 11 – Independent Ulyssa 98

Chapter 12 – Loving Lora 108

About the Authors 116

$\mathcal{F}$orward

As Charles Dickens once said, "It was the best of times, it was the worst of times, …it was the spirit of hope, the winter of despair." One could often say the same about the mother-in-law and daughter-in-law relationship. Sometimes two women tied together by marriage can have the best or worst of all their relationship has to offer. And it can be filled with hope or so desperately full of despair that all concerned suffer.

Wouldn't it be wonderful to have a mother-in-law like Naomi in the Old Testament book of Ruth? What an incredible woman of kindness, caring, selflessness, and amazing love. But even more importantly, she was a true witness to the reality of God to both of her daughters-in-law.

Or how about a daughter-in-law like Ruth? Now that would be a young woman filled with love and boundless loyalty, not only for her mother-in-law, but her mother-in-law's whole family.

With all the differences between the cultures of these two women that could have driven them apart we see instead a sweet and powerful story of women bound through love – for each other and for God. As the story develops and the relationship deepens, God is tremendously glorified and Naomi and Ruth are blessed in their present lives. Ultimately, as we all know, Ruth would become part of the family line through which the Messiah would come to redeem the world. God truly honored both women's obedience, loyalty, and love.

But, you say, this is the 21st Century and things sure are not like that now. The relationship has all too often become adversarial with both women competing for top place in the heart of one man who is both son and husband. Even God's women struggle every day to walk in the Spirit and have victory in this area. How can we grow in this ordained relationship and set an example for the world that God would be pleased with?

For mothers-in-law, it seems God's desire is for us to make it our business to find a place in our hearts for this woman of our son's choosing. He loves her just the WAY SHE IS and so must we. No two families are alike. We all come at life from different upbringings. But the mother-in-law's job is to love her son's wife – not to change her to be like her own family. We are to love her and reveal God to her through our love – as Naomi did to Ruth.

For daughters-in-law, the challenge is to love this woman who has parented her husband. That woman has often been the one who instilled spirituality and character and love into the head of her hopefully godly home. She is older, more mature, and life has taught her many valuable lessons which, if she is a godly woman, she is biblically commanded to pass on.

The many and varied stories in this book will reveal true and personal sagas of the rift that sadly develops in this precarious bond. Surely God has a better plan. And that is what this book is all about: Growing and developing roots and depth in our Christian homes and loving those God has chosen to give us in our extended families. What an opportunity we have as Christians to strive to change our world – relationship by relationship – and to see the love of Christ poured out in our families.

–In-Law and Bible Teacher, Lynne Ballard

Introduction

When the idea for this book began, we tossed it around and played with it only to put it aside – again and again. But no matter how hard we tried, stories flooded into our lives and the topic began to be impossible to ignore. So as God slowly opened our hearts and ears to the mother and daughter-in-law relationship, we realized that occasionally the stories were happy, but mostly they were incredibly painful. Sometimes we only heard the pain because the stories were too heartbreaking to tell.

So, impressed by the impact of this relationship on the lives of women, we began our journey to understand the problems encountered in this forced and touchy union. We began to research what was known and found out there wasn't a lot of formal research to pull from. So we gathered what we could and began to really talk to both mothers and daughters-in-law. Our chapters evolved out of problematic themes that emerged.

Next we began to search God's word and this time our research led to an abundance of instruction on these emerging problems. We began to understand, however, that the solutions the Bible offered began with the woman-God relationship. That relationship had to be set straight before the mother and daughter-in-law relationship could be positively affected. Then we realized that since only God can change a life, a mother-in-law was pretty much powerless to change her daughter-in-law and a daughter-in-law should not have high hopes for changing her mother-in-law.

From the idea that positive relationship change between a mother and daughter-in-law must begin with relationship change between one in-law and God, our underlying assumption, and the one that seems to work from a biblical standpoint, was formed. That assumption is, "One in-law has no control over the other in-law's motives, thoughts, feelings, or actions. One in-law can only acknowledge her own sins, bring her own thoughts captive to Christ, and let Him do the restorative work needed to be done." In short, only God can change you, and only God can change your in-law.

And so, our primary goal in this book is to get you to look at the motives, thoughts, and actions that drive interaction with your in-law and to see if these motives, thoughts, and actions are godly. If they are not, it is our desire that you would come to a place of repentance so God can restore you to the place in His kingdom He intended for you before you were born and so that you can take pleasure in Him and reflect His beauty and magnificence to the world around you – and that includes your in-law. And we believe that through this reflection of God by way of your good words and good deeds towards your in-law, she will be drawn to Him (Matthew 5:16). **And as you and your in-law draw closer to God, you will inevitably draw closer to each other.** The diagram on the following page demonstrates this principle.

Diagram Principle:
Draw Close To God & See God Move You Closer to Each Other

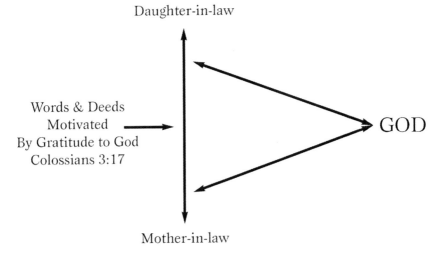

Daughter-in-law

Words & Deeds
Motivated
By Gratitude to God
Colossians 3:17

GOD

Mother-in-law

While this result, a close and peaceful mother and daughter-in-law relationship, is our hope, we realize no matter how diligently you put the teaching in this book into practice; it may never come about since the result depends on the cooperation of both women with God. We do believe, however, as you turn from ungodly behavior and move closer to God, He will provide the resources of peace, love, patience, gentleness, self-control, and joy to you so you can give a God-reflecting response to your in-law in any situation (Galatians 5:22).

About half of the mothers-in-law surveyed said they usually search the Bible for wisdom to solve problems with their daughters-in-law while only about one-third of daughters-in-law said they do the same. Age of the daughter-in-law did not make a difference. Mothers-in-law are also three times more likely than daughters-in-law to try and learn something from their in-law. On the other hand, daughters-in-law are ten percent more likely to seek advice about in-law problems from a godly person.

DAUGHTER-IN-LAW QUOTE: *Before I speak to my in-law about a sensitive issue, I "talk to my husband for advice on how to handle the situation."*

MOTHER-IN-LAW QUOTE: *When I pray about my in-law, I usually ask God, "to give her wisdom in all her many tasks."*

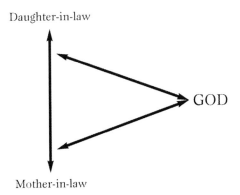

Wise Whitney

Real wisdom, God's wisdom, begins with a holy life and is characterized by getting along with others. It is gentle and reasonable, overflowing with mercy and blessings, not hot one day and cold the next, not two-faced. You can develop a healthy, robust community that lives right with God and enjoy its results only if you do the hard work of getting along with each other, treating each other with dignity and honor (James 3: 17-18, The Message).

Daughter-in-law's Side

"I told her not to buy them anything," Whitney complained to Josh as she walked in the door with Silas and Bret, who had his new airplane in tow. "The boys have too many toys already. Katie's always spoiling them. We were in the grocery store just yesterday, and Bret was begging for that same airplane. Despite his pleas and tears, I told him, 'No!' Now what does your mother do? She goes right out and gets him the very thing I told him he couldn't have.

And she is already training Silas to think he can have whatever he wants too. You should have seen her trying to slip the toothbrush she bought him into her bathroom. Believe me! I know the toothbrush was for Silas because it had a red car on it. He reaches out and says, 'please, please, please' at any red thing he sees," Whitney demonstrated, opening and closing her fist with each please. "And I certainly don't think your mother brushes her teeth with red car toothbrushes," Whitney added to make her point. "I know she wants the boys to love her, but does she really have to buy their love? It's like she lives to undermine all my training and make me out to look like the bad guy.

I hate feeling like this about Katie," Whitney thought later as she watched Josh toss the ball to Bret and then roll it to Silas. "I feel Josh tense up and pout every time I rant and rave about his mom. For Josh and for the boys' sake, I want to get along. But every time I leave Katie's I feel confused and irritated. She's always ready to help me with the boys when I need to drop them by. She always seems interested in me. So why won't she cooperate with me?"

Whitney watched the back and forth of the ball. "It's all so confusing. Confusion... what's that verse? Something about confusion being the result of envy and self-seeking. Am I seeking my own way? Is there something about Katie I'm not considering? What am I missing?"

Mother-in-law's Side

"Whitney gave me strict orders not to buy the kids anything," Katie confided to her friend, Marcie. "But every time she drops the boys off, she never brings anything for them to play with. Once when she was complaining about the excess of toys the boys have, I mentioned that maybe she could bring some of the toys to my house for the boys when they come over. I guess she forgot.

Bret has a great imagination so it's easy for me to make up stories for him to act out. They both enjoy books and thankfully I have plenty of those. Silas, the baby, loves to swing but, after a while, I get pretty tired. Yesterday I had to go to the grocery store to pick up some milk and juice for the boys. Talk about an exhausting activity - I don't know how Whitney does it with a four-year-old and a toddler. I remember I always dreaded the grocery store experience when my kids were small and they were five years apart. Of course right there, by the juice boxes, hung some toy planes. I know I shouldn't have, but Bret was begging and Silas was whining for the juice, so I gave in and got it. Since I was buying Bret the plane, I needed to get Silas something. I thought it would be a good thing to get him a toothbrush since he didn't have one at my house. He seemed excited over the one with the red car, so I grabbed it and the milk and made a beeline for the cash register.

I meant for the plane to stay at my house so Bret would have it to play with next time he comes over, but he clung to it so desperately. What could I do but let him have it and apologize to Whitney? I could tell by the look on her face she was furious with me. And she was in such a hurry to get the boys and go, I couldn't explain."

God's Angle - Two Types of Wisdom

There are two types of wisdom James reminds you - counterfeit earthly wisdom and true heavenly wisdom. These two types of wisdom come from different sources and have very different outcomes in your life. In fact, you can recognize the type of wisdom you are using and the source it comes from by noticing the outcomes in your life. Read James 3:13-18, in several versions if possible, and consider the following summary.

Counterfeit earthly wisdom has three sources:
- human reasoning separated from God's influence
- human sensory information
- evil

Outcomes produced by counterfeit earthly wisdom are
- jealousy/envy
- contention/rivalry/selfish ambition/mean-spiritedness
- confusion/unrest/disharmony/rebellion
- evil and despicable habits

People using counterfeit wisdom are inclined to
- boast about their wisdom
- try to make themselves look better than others
- twist the truth to make themselves look wise

True heavenly wisdom has one source:
- God, who is truth

Outcomes of true wisdom are

- peacefulness
- courteousness/considerateness/gentleness
- submissiveness to God's word/ willingness to obey
- compassion/mercy
- impartiality/open-mindedness
- authenticity/truthfulness/sincerity/steadfastness

People who use true heavenly wisdom have a desire to

- be gracious towards others
- have an unpretentious nature
- be involved in good works
- treat others with dignity and honor
- inspire others to live right before God

Whitney is relying on counterfeit earthly wisdom. We can conclude this by evaluating the outcomes in her life. For example, contention and rivalry are apparent in Whitney's idea that Katie is trying to make her out "to look like the bad guy." It is also clear from the story that Whitney is feeling confused and angry over Katie's seemingly rebellious attitude toward her rules.

Where are You on the Triangle?
Reflect on your relationship with your in-law and honestly answer the following.

1. What complaints, feelings, and attitudes do you have about your in-law?
2. Which outcomes, previously listed, are evident in your relationship with your in-law?
3. Are these outcomes mainly the result of Counterfeit Wisdom or of True Wisdom?

Finding God's Perspective
Use a Bible to help you answer the questions below.

1. Identify the source of true wisdom.
   a. 1 Kings 10: 24

b. Job 12: 13

c. Proverbs 2: 6

2. Identify the source of counterfeit wisdom.

   a. James 3: 14-16

   b. Proverbs 3: 7

3. The fear of the Lord is related to true wisdom. What does it mean to fear the Lord? Why is fear of the Lord a necessary first step?

   a. Job 28: 28

   b. Psalm 111: 10

4. Who can get true wisdom?

   a. James 1: 5

5. Counterfeit wisdom is the type of wisdom you naturally depend on? You have to consciously make a decision to rely on God's true wisdom. What steps must you take to become really wise?

   a. Proverbs 1: 7

   b. 2 Chronicles 9: 7

   c. Proverbs 2: 1-12

6. It is easy to fall back into the habit of using counterfeit wisdom. Based on the scriptures above and your personal habits, name three things you will have to continually do to maintain true wisdom in your life?

7. How will people recognize true wisdom in you?

   a. Deuteronomy 4: 5-7

8. How will your life be changed when you use true wisdom rather than counterfeit wisdom?

   a. Proverbs 3: 13

   b. Proverbs 4: 8

9. Counterfeit wisdom is the wisdom generally relied on by most people – even Christians. Identify someone you know who relies on true wisdom. How are the outcomes of true wisdom noticeable in this person's life?

Note: Think about what this person says and how this person behaves.

10. Give an example of how using true wisdom will change your relationship with your in-law?

Trust God to Make the Move

What happened to Whitney? You saw her recognize her confusion over, what on the surface appeared to be, Katie's defiance. After this first step - recognizing an outcome of counterfeit wisdom in her life-she eventually began to seek true wisdom, God's word, to help her. God promises to give wisdom to those who ask (James 1: 5). Using God's word to guide her, Whitney eventually learned to rely on God's wisdom even when it didn't make sense to her. At first depending on God's wisdom was hard because it didn't feel normal and usually led her to behave in ways that felt unnatural and uncomfortable since God's wisdom usually is at odds with human nature. But as she saw God work in many of her relationships including the one with her mother-in-law, she began to trust and use His wisdom more and more. Change didn't happen overnight but, more quickly than you would think, everyone could tell Whitney's character had changed.

Peacefulness grew when Whitney made a purposeful decision to trust God to work out impasses and to force good and true thoughts of Katie to dominate her thinking.

Courteousness, considerateness, and gentleness increased when Whitney began to thoughtfully inquire about Katie's needs when she dropped the boys off, and to follow-up with conversations of the day's events when she picked the boys up.

Submissiveness to God's word and a willingness to obey began when Whitney made a commitment to study Proverbs. As she read she confessed her sins and prayed for the kind of wisdom God wanted her to have and use. Her commitment to true wisdom enabled Whitney to love Katie even when Katie made it difficult.

Compassion and mercy became easier because Whitney remembered how God had forgiven her when she was less than perfect. As a result she found it easier to extend compassion and mercy to Katie.

Impartiality and open-mindedness became key in Whitney and Katie's relationship. Using open-minded conversations, Whitney determined to investigate Katie's motives before jumping to wrong conclusions and often found that Katie had reasonable explanations for her behavior.

Authenticity, truthfulness, sincerity, and steadfastness began to define Whitney and Katie's relationship when Whitney decided to be open and honest with Katie about her feelings.

Try This:

For each word or phrase below, list some specific ways you can use God's wisdom so these outcomes will begin to characterize your relationship with your in-law:

1. *Peacefulness*
2. *Courteousness, considerateness, and gentleness*
3. *Submissiveness to God's word and willingness to obey*
4. *Compassion and mercy*
5. *Impartiality and open-mindedness*
6. *Authenticity, truthfulness, sincerity, and steadfastness*

King Solomon tells us, *"Through skillful and godly wisdom is a house (a life, a home, a family) built, and by understanding it is established [on a sound and good foundation], and by knowledge shall its chambers [of every area] be filled with all precious and pleasant riches"* (Proverbs 24: 3, Amplified Bible). So, you can know that as you grow in truth and knowledge of God, the outcomes of true wisdom will be established in your life.

An Ending Thought

"I do not want the peace that passeth understanding. I want the understanding which bringeth peace."

–Helen Keller

Seventy-one percent of mothers-in-law and sixty-three percent of daughters-in-law surveyed are aware of their in-law's likes and dislikes. And over ninety percent of mothers and daughters-in-law said they try to make time together as pleasant as possible.

DAUGHTER-IN-LAW QUOTE: *When my in-law upsets me "I try to overlook it and be accepting and a little less opinionated than in years past."*

MOTHER-IN-LAW QUOTE: *My comments about my in-law are often, "not as positive as they should be."*

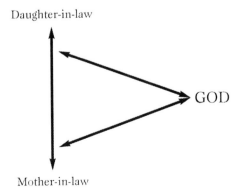

Patient Patty

But those that wait on the Lord shall renew their strength; they shall mount up with wings like eagles, they shall run and not grow weary, they shall walk and not faint (Isaiah 40: 31, New King James Version).

Daughter-in-law's Side

Jeff and Patty were married when she was twenty-nine. His mother, Jackie, was frigid towards Patty during her courtship with Jeff. Patty set out to remedy that situation soon after they moved to Jacksonville. She very much wanted Jackie's approval. She wanted Jackie to think she was a "good choice" for Jeff. And she wanted Jeff to be proud of her. So it seemed that securing the blessing of her mother-in-law would cement her place as a praiseworthy wife.

Patty had always had a wonderful relationship with her own mother. She considered her to be her most trustworthy friend and greatest cheerleader. She fully understood she wouldn't be able to create that same kind of mother-daughter bond with Jackie. But still, at the very least, Patty wanted Jackie to like her, to enjoy her company, and to be glad she was now a part of her family. But she felt somewhat intimidated by Jackie and uncertain that she would be able to win her approval.

Looking back, Patty believes that in her interactions with Jackie, she unknowingly made some erroneous assumptions. Patty thinks now that a little bit of analytical thinking would have revealed that to her.

One of her primary presumptions was that Jackie would respond to her in the same supportive manner her own mom did. Nothing could have been further from reality. The first example of this contrast came shortly after Jeff and Patty moved into their new home.

Patty had worked hard on their little bungalow. She had thoughtfully chosen paint colors and decorated it in what she thought was a warm and friendly way. She used pottery, books, and pictures throughout the living area. She thought of it as a "honeymoon cottage" and she loved it! But then one day, when Jackie came over for a visit she told Patty about an antebellum home she has just visited with her Architect Review Chapter. She commented that the home was "the most cluttered, dismal place she'd ever seen." Then, looking around Patty's living room, she added, "But I'm sure you would have loved it." Patty couldn't have been more surprised than if Jackie had slapped her in the face.

Years later as Patty sat thinking about her relationship with Jackie, it occurred to her how different their tastes were. Patty enjoyed warm colors. Jackie preferred cool blues and whites. Patty's coffee table had candlesticks, a stack of five books, and numerous pictures. Jackie's coffee table had a contemporary glass top with a solitary ceramic apple atop a single abstract-art book.

It took Patty quite a while to realize that different tastes in coffee tables didn't translate into personal disapproval. It has also taken years for her to realize that what Jackie thinks, she speaks, whether it's gentle or not. Patty eventually noticed that trait is dominant in all Jackie's relationships. Patty convinced herself that Jackie's directness is the result of her architectural career since she has dealt with building contractors all of her professional life and must speak her mind – clearly and unequivocally. Unlike Patty's mother, who acknowledges something positive even if she would have done it completely differently, Jackie doesn't sugar coat anything - with Patty or anyone else.

Patty has observed that daughters-in-law hear their mothers-in-law so differently. In those early years it never occurred to Patty that Jackie's candid, straightforward nature was not directed at her. In contrast, Patty believed Jackie was being harsh and overly critical; when in fact, she was treating Patty like she did everyone else.

Armed with the understanding of Jackie's direct approach, Patty realizes now she could have saved herself from numerous disappointments by refraining from asking Jackie opinion questions. In an effort to begin a conversation with Jackie, Patty would often ask Jackie her opinion of food, travel, people, and so forth, all the while subconsciously expecting a soft, small-talk kind of answer. "But Jackie never did small talk," Patty confessed. "I should have never asked her a question unless I wanted her true opinion!" For instance, on one particular birthday meal Patty had prepared a seafood casserole steeped in cream and cheese. She asked Jackie's opinion before placing it on the table. Jackie abruptly said, "I don't like food disguised with heavy sauces." On another occasion, Patty and Jeff asked Jackie's professional opinion of a new home they wanted to buy. Jeff said, "Do you like it, Mama?" She tartly replied, "Well, it's okay if you like low ceilings and dark spaces."

Upon reflection, Patty thinks she set her own self up for failure by expecting a certain kind of response from Jackie that never happened. Then when Jackie gave a blatantly honest response, Patty became angry or hurt.

As time passed, Patty gave up trying to please her mother-in-law and just tried to love and accept her. And today, those traits of decisiveness and directness are traits that Patty has learned to admire in many ways. If she needs to make arrangements for anything, dealing with Jackie is a breeze. If Jackie commits to a plan, Patty can consider it done. If Jackie says she likes something, there is no need to wonder if she is just being nice. There is absolutely no beating around the bush about anything.

Patty has also realized Jackie's lack of desire for a "chummy" relationship has its perks. While other wives complain of in-laws interfering in their lives by dropping in or calling incessantly, Jackie is very non-intrusive. She has not dropped in on Patty once in eleven years of marriage. When Patty doesn't comply with Jackie's wishes, Jackie doesn't pout, give her the silent treatment, or show disapproval in any other way. Jackie does what she wants to do and seems to respect Jeff and Patty's choices.

"A lasting benefit," Patty explains, "that results from Jackie's direct and practical nature is this – she trained a terrific husband. In fact, Jackie could write a book about creating a responsible, neat, independent life partner. There are no 'woman's' house duties and 'man's' house duties with a child of Jackie's. A man under her guidance respects women, is very thick-skinned, and in no way expects to be waited on."

Mother-in-law's Side

Jackie and her husband worked very hard in their professions. As intelligent educated people, training their children to be independent productive adults was of utmost importance. They were concerned about the image their family presented in the community and presumed their children would choose the same church, bank, cars, homes, and way of life they had chosen. Up until his marriage, Jeff had gone along with his parents' choices out of respect.

But after his marriage to Patty, Jeff began making choices that Jackie did not understand or agree with. In his mind, Jeff was implementing the biblical principle of leaving his mother and father and joining with his wife to become one flesh which meant making decisions with Patty for the best interests of his new family. This idea was beyond Jackie's independent thinking, and though she loved her son, Jackie allowed Jeff's conviction to create a great chasm between her and her son. And unknown to Patty, it was the root of her frigidness towards Patty. Jackie had no desire to bend or seek God's direction for reconciliation.

Jackie's first reaction to Jeff's change in direction was worry over how his choices would affect her image. It was impossible for her to accept all the decisions Jeff and Patty made. She felt they made a poor choice when they decided to join a church whose membership lacked influential people. She strongly disagreed with their decision to home school. And Jackie thought their choice of neighborhoods was poorly made.

She dug her heels in and what she interpreted as their defiance definitely became an issue. She would often give Jeff the cold-shoulder treatment and, at times, she would just break off communication completely. It was easier for her not to communicate than to get in an argument with Jeff.

God's Angle – Waiting Patiently

Waiting on the Lord sounds easy but, for believers, sometimes it seems almost unbearable. Waiting requires you to exhibit character traits approved of by God. *"Wait for the Lord; be strong and take heart and wait for the Lord,"* (Psalm 27: 14, New International Version) the psalmist challenges. Waiting involves trust, patience, and faith.

Trusting means believing the Lord is in control and has your best interests in mind. It is the belief He is working for your good in order to reveal Himself as God through you to others for their good (Romans 8: 28). It is the understanding that it is His pleasure to bring about good in your life and in your in-law's life Because each time a life is turned from bad to good, God's purpose of pointing others to Himself as Lord is fulfilled (Ephesians 1: 5-6). In other words God wants to transform both you and your in-law into His likeness in order to show others, through you, who Christ truly is (2 Corinthians 3: 17-18). So, He encourages you to be joyful in hope, patient in difficulties (James 2: 2-4), and faithful in prayer so you will have peace and others will be drawn to Christ through your joy.

Waiting Patiently requires two things. First it means placing your confidence in God. Doing that allows Him to produce a quiet calmness in you. Rather than fretting about circumstances, people, and things going on around you, you will be seeking His direction and trusting Him to provide it.

Second, waiting patiently also requires you to examine your circumstances from God's perspective which means you have to understand the true character and purposes of God; that's where lots of Bible study comes in handy. Seeing situations from God's point of view, allows you to notice where He is at work and what action you should take. Delays in progress with your in-law relationship present you with opportunities to react in ways that display God's character to your in-law and the world around you. Your in-law will be able see what the transforming power of Jesus has accomplished in you. Your behavior will invite your in-law to move closer to Jesus.

Walking by Faith is not a sight walk. You will be required to think and act in ways that will not be in your comfort zone. God will prompt you to use His wisdom and love as a guide for your actions. He will expect you to do things His way rather than your way. But as you wait patiently for Him, He will go before you and give you direction (Proverbs 3: 6). This is where Bible study comes in handy again since, *"faith comes by hearing, and hearing by the word of God"* (Romans 10: 17, New King James Version). You must have the kind of faith that allows you to trust God even without knowing when or how He will resolve a situation.

As Jeff and Patty trust, wait patiently, and walk by faith, God will make His righteousness shine in their life like the dawn and the noonday sun (Psalm 37: 3-8).

Where are You on the Triangle?

The Lord's perspective of waiting is very different for most peoples'. We may experience delays or see obstacles. But He says those that wait on Him will be blessed (Isaiah 30: 18).

Reflect on your relationship with your in-law and honestly answer the following.

1. Do you see your times of waiting as an opportunity to show your in-law how you can love her in spite of your differences?
2. Would others say you are standing firm in your faith, being

still, and waiting patiently for God to work in your
circumstances?

Finding God Perspective

Use a Bible to help you answer the questions below.

1. Is it possible for you to rest in the Lord? Resting in the Lord
   does not depend on outside circumstances but on your
   relationship with Him. Would you say you are resting or
   wrestling with the Lord?
   a. Psalm 37: 7

2. What does it mean to abide under the shadow of the
   Almighty? How will knowing God is your refuge and fortress
   help you when you feel hurt by your in-law's actions?
   a. Psalm 91: 1-2

3. How will the contentment the Apostle Paul speaks of affect
   the way you deal with your in-law problems?
   a. I Timothy 6: 6-8

4. What character qualities should you pursue and why?
   a. 1 Timothy 6: 11-12

5. After your study of these scriptures, how would you evaluate
   Patty's attitude toward her mother-in law?

6. As one of God's chosen, what should you put on? Even in
   disappointing circumstances what should your attitude be?

Trust God to Make the Move

The circumstances Jackie created were very hurtful. They were
painful for Jeff because he loved his mother very much and was
grateful for the time she spent caring for him. They were difficult for
Patty because she felt Jackie was rejecting her personally.

Patty and Jeff both wanted to honor God in their relationship with
Jackie and so they looked to His word for guidance. And as a result,
Patty is now walking in faith. She is no longer explaining away
Jackie's rudeness towards her as a stable character trait that can't be

changed. She is now waiting patiently and trusting God to turn Jackie's heart towards repentance and towards Him. She now sees her circumstances as stepping stones that will build perseverance and increase her faith. Patty understands the character traits God desires. She is trusting Him to accomplish change in her own life. She knows God is working for her good and believes His desire is to accomplish desirable character traits in Jackie also. It's a challenge for Patty and Jeff to accept Jackie as she is for now, to trust God, and to wait for Him to change hearts, but they both believe He is able.

Try This:

1. Write down three things related to your in-law relationship that you are anxious about. Write down your solution. Open your Bible and ask God to show you His solution. Don't leave until He does.

2. Identify a woman you know who patiently waits on God to change her circumstances. Name three character traits, not including patience, she possesses that God approves of and you admire. In addition to patience, ask God to manifest those traits in you.

An Ending Thought

"Faith enables us so to rejoice in the Lord so that our infirmities become platforms for the display of His grace."

-Evangelist, C.H. Spurgeon

Eighty-five percent of mothers-in-law surveyed said they pray for their daughter-in-law's best interests while only thirty-nine percent of daughters-in-law do the same for their mother-in-law. Similarly more than three-fourths of mothers-in-law said they encourage and praise their daughter-in-law while less than one-half of daughters-in-law surveyed do so for their mother-in-law.

DAUGHTER-IN-LAW QUOTE: *I wish my mother-in-law would "stop being so self-absorbed."*

MOTHER-IN-LAW QUOTE: *I wish I could convince my in-law "that demands and expectations aren't the best way to grow relationships."*

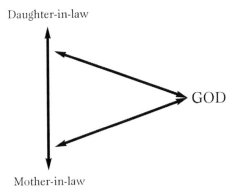

Selfish Sally

*T*he *righteous cry out, and the Lord hears, and delivers them out of all their troubles. The Lord is near to those who have a broken heart, and saves such as have a contrite spirit* (Psalm 34: 17-18, New King James Version).

Daughter-in-law's Side

Heartbroken and sobbing, Betty slowly sat down at the kitchen table. She could hear Eddie's car backing out of the driveway. Then silence. The house seemed empty and cold. She shuddered at the thought of being alone. She was stunned by what she had just heard.

"I can't believe this is happening to me," thought Betty, "a divorce! After twenty-four years of marriage, Eddie wants out. I thought that we had a good marriage. I know we have terrible financial problems. But all marriages have problems - right?

I guess my mother-in-law is finally happy. She wanted this to happen since day one. She spoiled my wedding day by refusing to come to our wedding. Only Eddie's brother, who was probably sent there to report on the event, represented his family.

But we had a beautiful wedding and reception anyway. My mom and dad wanted us to enjoy our celebration and were very supportive. All our other relatives and friends were there, and so, despite Sally's boycott, it was a happy day.

I began married life with Eddie thinking, as time went by, everything would work out with my new-in-laws. I wasn't at all prepared for the verbal abuse and constant criticism from my mother-in-law that followed.

I think I could have coped with Sally's cruelty and disapproval better if Eddie had stood up for me. But, he never did. Evidently he was afraid to take my side on any issue. Seems like those wedding vows had a line saying, 'Forsaking all others...' I guess that didn't mean Mama!

I'll have to admit Eddie's parents were very good to our two boys. When they were small, they bought Gary and Josh every toy they wanted. They still entice them with things even though they are both teen-agers now. They always enjoyed having my boys stay with them as much as possible. I never tried to keep my children away even though I never felt accepted myself.

I'm not trying to say I was perfect. But I was the one that did all the work around the house: I mowed the lawn, cooked good meals, and worked at various other jobs all our married life. Even with that, all in all, I thought my marriage was good. Not perfect, but good.

Eddie and I always had financial problems. Neither one of us was ever good at managing money or living within our means. My mother-in-law blamed me for that. Eddie was never the brunt of her criticism.

I always knew my mother-in-law wanted Eddie to leave me. Not too long ago, Sally said that she would pay for a divorce if he would get one. She told me the boys were old enough to choose who they wanted to live with—me or their father. I guess my mistake was just walking away, not choosing to confront her.

I love Eddie, and I thought we were happy. I know there isn't another woman—except his mother! What could I have done to prevent this sad ending to our marriage? I wish I had remained faithful to my beliefs about God. My parents always took me to church and encouraged Eddie and me to go. He never wanted to. I really need prayer now."

Mother-in-law's Side

"Well, I guess Eddie finally realized we've been right all these

years about that wife of his," concluded Sally. "Now, he can be free
from that financial mess Betty got him into. He and the boys will get
along just fine, that is if we can talk Gary and Josh into leaving with
their dad too. We'll buy them a house and help out financially until
Eddie can get a better job."

"Whatever you think is best," Sam responded. "But you know
Sally, Betty will insist on a settlement. After all, she'll lose the house
because she can't make the house payment. And no payment has been
made in several months. She works two jobs. I wonder what she does
with all that money."

"Well, our son really won't have anything to give her!" Sally
retorted. "Not on his salary. We'll have to get a good attorney who
will understand the situation. We'll help him all we can. It will be
so good to have Eddie back with us, and we can take good care of him
just like we do his brother. At least our other son had the good sense
not to ever marry that girl he was dating."

"Yes, sweetie-pie, we'll have both of our boys," agreed Sam, "and
hopefully both our grandsons will see how much more we have to
offer them too. Eventually we'll all be one happy family. But, you
know, somehow I don't think we're doing Betty right. She's a good
mother, a wonderful cook, and a good housekeeper. You have to give
her credit for that," Sam reminded Sally.

"I don't have to give her credit for anything!" snapped Sally.
"Finally, we have Eddie back where he belongs. "I never wanted him
to get married. But he thought he was in love and wouldn't listen to
me. Maybe now, without all that responsibility, he'll be able to enjoy
a stress-free life." Giving her husband a contented look, Sally left the
room.

God's Angle - Selfish Desires

Then Jesus said to His disciples, "If anyone desires to come after me, let
him deny himself, and take up his cross, and follow me." For whoever
desires to save his life will lose it, and whoever loses his life for my sake will

find it" (Matt.16:24-25, New King James Version).

Let Go

When you observe the actions of a selfish in-law, you will probably notice she insists you give into her wants regardless of how they affect you. God teaches that if you really want to make your life count in this world, you must give up everything for Him – and that includes people you love.

If you truly love someone, you have to be willing to let them go. Allow that person to live his or her life and trust God for the results. If it's your son you're letting go of in marriage, look for the good in your in-law. Ask God to help you to see her "best" side. You can do it!

Grow up

We are born selfish. Infants, as soon as they learn to use their little hands, reach for glasses, jewelry, or any other object within their grasp. Some in-laws never grow up. Like infants, they try to hang on to what or who they consider to be their own. Are you one of those selfish in-laws? Does God condone your actions?

Do you remember this story written in the Bible about how Solomon, the wisest man, solved a difficult problem? This story reveals the love of a mother for her new-born child.

King Solomon was approached by two women, each claiming to be the mother of a new born baby. One of the babies had accidentally been smothered during the night. Since the two women shared the same house, one of them had placed the dead baby in the other's bed and claimed the baby that was alive belonged to her. How did Solomon, who had been given the gift of wisdom, solve the problem?

Solomon asked for a sword. He gave an order for the baby to be cut in half and to give half to one mother and half to the other. Immediately the real mother, who loved her son so much, told the king, *"Please, my lord, give her the living baby, don't kill him."* But the other woman said, *"Neither I nor you shall have him. Cut him in two."* Then King Solomon knew the real mother was the one who wanted her baby's life spared. So he gave her the baby (1 Kings 3: 16-28, New

International Version).

Do you love enough to "let go?"

Obey God

"Let all bitterness, wrath, anger, clamor, and evil speaking be put away from you, with all malice. And be kind to one another, tenderhearted, forgiving one another, just as God in Christ also forgave you" (Ephesians 4: 31, 32, New King James Version).

"For this reason a man shall leave his father and mother and be joined to his wife, and the two shall become one flesh" (Matthew 19:5, New King James Version). *"This is a great mystery, but I speak concerning Christ and the church. Nevertheless let each one of you in particular so love his own wife as himself, and let the wife see that she respects her husband"* (Ephesians 5: 31-33, New King James Version).

God teaches us to follow His ways and trust in Him, no matter what the circumstances are that you are facing today. Do you have a decision to make?

Where are You on the Triangle?

Reflect on your relationship with your in-law and honestly answer the following.

1. What are the underlying causes of your problem with the "other" woman? Are they the result of selfish desires?
2. You have always heard that there are two sides to every problem. Do you honestly believe that's true in your situation?
3. Do you "give in" or "give out?" Have you "given up?" What has your selfish attitude solved?
4. What things/people are difficult for you to let go of?
5. Everyone has selfish desires. Have you honestly acknowledged yours to the Lord?

Finding God's Perspective

Use a Bible to help you answer the questions below.

1. If you have put to death your selfish desires, what will the

outcome be?

a. Galatians 5: 16-26

2. Why do you think God commands a man, once married, to leave his father and mother?

a. Genesis 2: 24

b. Matthew 19: 4-6

3. Should you spend time thinking about how to solve a problem with a selfish in-law?

a. Proverbs 3: 5, 6

4. God is not selfish. He has a wonderful gift for you. Have you accepted His gift?

a. Ephesians 2: 8, 9

Trust God to Make the Move

While Betty realizes that her sons depend on her, she also knows they love their grandparents. So Betty determined not to cause more heartache for them by "bad-mouthing" her in-laws or their father. She longs for the whole ordeal "to be over." She prays that she can handle the heartache that has been dealt her in a way pleasing to God, but she is broken in spirit.

What about you? Are you troubled, perplexed, and sad? Perhaps you really can't see a solution to your problems. What is the next step? At times you may feel like a hypocrite because you wonder if God is even aware of your situation. Satan enjoys that type of thinking. But, listen. Do you realize that you are so special to God He has your name engraved in the palm of His hand (Isaiah 49: 15-16)?

Try This:

1. No situation is beyond God's control. Whether you identify with Betty or Sally, God's plan is always best. And sometimes His plan includes consequences to be endured. As you deal with selfish desires in your in-law relationship:

   • Ask God to show you your own selfishness. Ask Him to help you forgive your in-law for her self-centeredness. Ask

God to give you guidance as you deal with your in-law's self-absorption.

• Yield yourself completely to God. Ask God to let His desires become your desires.

2. Think about God by using today's method of communication and be amazed at how the Lord will work in your in-law relationship:

www.faith.com

Wait	for the Lord to work in you and in your in-law (Psalm 27: 14; Psalm 33: 20).
Worship	the Lord with a joyful heart no matter what your situation is with your in-law (Psalm 100: 1-4).
Work,	God's work, in you will result in lasting peace, quietness, and confidence (Isaiah 32: 17).
Faith	results in rewards (Hebrews 11: 6) .com

An Ending Thought

"In a textile factory, a sign over the machines read, 'When the threads get tangled, send for the foreman.' One day the threads got tangled on one machine, and the operator tried desperately to untangle them. Just then the foreman came along and asked, 'Don't you see the sign?'

'Yes,' was the reply, 'but I'm doing my best to take care of it myself.'

'Doing the best you can always means sending for the foreman,' the foreman responded.

Doing our best with life's tangled problems means calling on the Great Overseer."

-Evangelist and author, Vance Havner

Prayer

Thank you, Father, for caring so much for me. I know I am your child and You want what is best for me and my family. Forgive me for my lack of trust in You. Rekindle my spirit with Your love as I wait on You. Cleanse me of my selfish desires.

-Amen

Over half of mothers-in-law and about seventy-five percent of daughters-in-law say their in-law, at least sometimes, makes insensitive remarks. But are these remarks really insensitive or are they misinterpreted. About sixty-five percent of both mothers and daughters-in-law say that, at least sometimes, their in-law misinterprets ordinary remarks they make.

It is also interesting to note seventy-one percent of mothers-in-law and forty-one percent of daughters-in-law who describe their relationship as above average say they can openly and honestly express their feelings with their in-law. None of the mothers and daughters-in-law, who describe their relationship as below average, said they could.

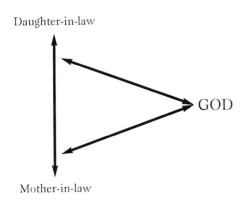

Overly-Sensitive Olivia

Do not say what is wrong in other people's lives. Then other people will not say what is wrong in your life. Do not say someone is guilty. Then other people will not say you are guilty. Forgive other people and other people will forgive you (Luke 6: 37, New Life Version).

Daughter-in-law's Side

"I feel pretty confident I'm a good wife and mom until my crazy mother-in-law shows up. The other day when Victoria dropped Caleb off, she said, "I put some Caladryl Lotion on ALL those mosquito bites on his legs in case you wonder why his legs are pink." She's always implying that I'm a bad mom – that I don't take care of Caleb properly. And, by the way, I put CLEAR Caladryl on him – so of course she doesn't even notice that.

That same day, Victoria, that's my mother-in-law's name, went into Caleb's room to put his overnight bag down and started picking up toys and dirty clothes. I had just finished cleaning the entire house except for his room, and was just about to clean it, before she arrived. If she had only waited thirty more minutes, it would have been spotless. She's always doing stuff like that. She doesn't say anything but I can tell by the look on her face she disapproves of my housecleaning. I teach all week long, grade papers, call parents at night, and get lesson plans together on the weekend. What does she expect my house to look like? What does she do all week? Probably nothing! No wonder her house is always spotless. It's like a museum - you'd think nobody actually lived there.

And she's always making comments about Matt's clothes. I've

asked him a million times not to wear those nasty wrinkled t-shirts he's had since he was eighteen over to his mom's. I think he just does it on purpose to irritate her, but it ends up making me look like I'm not doing my 'wifely duty' of caring for him. Actually, Matt IS in charge of the clothes. He even irons my clothes for work because he's a better ironer than me. But I would never dare tell Victoria that. I'm sure she would disapprove. She disapproves of everything else."

Mother-In-Law's Side

"For some reason, whenever I'm around Olivia, I feel like I'm always displeasing her. She's always pouting around me and won't tell me what's wrong. It's like I have to think through everything I do so that I don't upset her. And usually, no matter what I do, it always turns out to be the wrong thing. At least that's what the information I get from Matt implies. It's like she picks apart everything I say or do.

I really like Olivia and I try to be as sensitive to her feelings as I possibly can. But honestly, I feel like giving up on ever having the kind of easy and peaceful relationship I would like to have with her. I really don't think I'll ever be able to say or do anything without offending her in one way or another.

Matt says Olivia thinks I'm always judging her. Well I honestly don't understand that. I'm totally bewildered about how to make my relationship with Olivia work. I'm so confused about all this I could cry."

And she did - uncontrollably.

God's Angle – Overly Sensitive Feelings

For every national catastrophe there are first responders like the National Guard or the fire department. And for every relationship catastrophe there are first responses. Consider these responses when your in-law offends you, hurts your feelings, or insults you.

Response #1: Arm yourself and stand firm. Put on the breastplate of righteousness so you can stand warns the Apostle Paul in

Ephesians 6. Righteousness is the status of a person approved of by God. Who does God approve of? The God who created our vast universe – the God who wholeheartedly hates and opposes sin - approves of you when you understand, totally rely, and act on the fact that you can only have peace with Him because of the clean-up work Jesus did for you on the cross (Romans 4, 8). That means you can confidently stand in the perfect work of Christ and His righteousness – not on your own thoughts, words, and deeds (Romans 5: 1). Stop! Think deeply about that.

Aimless wandering people look to someone other than God for approval. Put on the breastplate of righteousness to protect your heart. Don't evaluate yourself by the opinions of others. If God is for you, then who can be against you (Romans 8: 31)?

And know that your in-law will not have a reason to have a bad opinion of you as God washes out the yucky stuff inside you. This is the second meaning of righteousness in the Ephesians 6 verse. When God assigns Jesus Christ's right standing to you, God the Spirit begins to transform your mind. Integrity, right thinking, right acting, and purity will begin to be evident within you and noticed by others. So, if or when your in-law slanders you, your good actions will prove her wrong and God will be glorified because of it (1 Peter 2: 12).

Response #2: Rely on a superior force. Matthew 5: 5 (King James Version) says, *"Blessed are the meek for they shall inherit the earth."* Meekness is trusting God, a far superior power, to fight for you without your help. Psalm 37 puts it this way; those who wait, hope and look for the Lord to defend and protect them, in the end, will own the entire earth and live in peace. Those who stay angry and upset all the time won't.

Another reason for asking and relying on God to fight for you is the nature of the enemy. The reason the Apostle Paul warns you to put on the breastplate of righteousness along with the other spiritual armor is because the enemy you fight against is not really your in-law. The enemy is the spirit(s) that is influencing, oppressing, or controlling your in-law (Ephesians 6: 12). If your in-law is not responding from God's power, love, a calm well-balanced mind, and disciplined self-control, then most likely the spirit that is influencing your in-law is not from God (2 Timothy 1: 7).

Response #3: Don't attack. Be careful not to make wrong assumptions about your in-law's motives. God has lots to say about attacks of false accusations, slander, evil speaking, lying, and whispering. Throughout the Bible, God strongly disapproves of assuming people. Proverbs 6 says there are six things God hates; one of them is a false witness who breathes out lies.

Lots of really outstanding people have been falsely accused. Jesus Himself was accused of being insane, having a demon, and being a wino among other things. So, don't be deceived by the evil one. And don't give into your own human desire to invent stories that will help you make a case against your in-law.

Olivia and Victoria are not using any of these three responses. They are not armed and standing firm since they are both looking to each other rather than to God for approval. Neither does it appear that they are relying on a superior force. They may be praying for God to intervene - but if they are, neither seems to really believe He will. And they are attacking one another since they are both making assumptions, whether true or false, about each other's feelings and motives. Victoria is probably right. If both women continue this pattern of thinking, they will never have a peaceful relationship.

Where are You on the Triangle?

Reflect on your relationship with your in-law and honestly answer the following.

1. Who do you look to for approval?
2. What is your first response when you feel attacked by your in-law?
3. How do you feel when you are misunderstood, misjudged, or when wrong assumptions are made about you?

4. How do think your in-law feels when you misunderstand, misjudge, and make wrong assumptions about her?

Finding God's Perspective
Use a Bible to help you answer the questions below.

1. Who does God approve of?
    a. Romans 3: 22-28
2. How does knowing God approves of you help you deal will the disapproval of your in-law?
3. Why should you stand still and trust God to fight for you?
    a. Isaiah 41: 9-11
    b. Proverbs 29: 25
4. Who is guilty of hurting others with words?
    a. James 3: 2
    b. Ecclesiastes 7: 20-22
5. In what ways may you have offended your in-law with your words?
6. Why should you carefully consider the words you speak about your in-law?
    a. Matthew 12: 35-37
    b. Ephesians 4: 29-32
    c. Exodus 23: 1, 7

Trust God to Make the Move
As Victoria buried her face in her bedroom rug and sobbed uncontrollably to God, a warmness, like a big hug surrounded her and the words, "I love you like I love my own son. I see you like I see him," trickled into her thoughts. In that moment she understood God valued her and a rush of peace and joy flooded Victoria's heart. That one moment gave her confidence that, to this day, continues to live in her heart. As a result, Victoria began to trust God to work out her relationship with Olivia. By asking God to renew her mind daily and remind her of how He saw her, she was able to refrain from drawing

negative conclusions about Olivia. Victoria also began to pray Olivia would find the same joy and peace she had. Without even being aware of it, Victoria began to reflect the calmness and delight that came from the confidence she had knowing she was a child of a good God she could trust.

And eventually, Olivia began to think about Victoria differently. Though she couldn't communicate why, a genuine love and respect for Victoria began to grow in Olivia's heart.

Try this:

1. If you have offended your in-law or if she has offended you, Jesus, in Matthew 5: 22-24, instructs you to make efforts to patch things up. He discusses the severe consequences for those who don't. Ask God to cleanse your heart and give you the words that He wants you to say to your in-law. Write His words.

2. Psalm 62: 5 is a reminder that when all your expectations rest on God, your soul will find peace. As your trust in God grows, you will not be so easily offended by the words and actions of your in-law. Be prepared. Prayerfully write 3 steps you will take the next time you are tempted to be offended.

An Ending Thought

"It's wasted time taken
to gaze into my heart
to see what's been forsaken.
Locked tight in bitter eyes
her iron wall's gate won't swing;
I despise this dire disguise.
Then Your warm tears fell near
and mercy I pleaded
as Your yearnings surfaced clear."

–Author, Rena Hill

NOTES

Almost three-fourths of the mothers-in-law surveyed said they admit their part in a disagreement while less than ten percent of daughters-in-law say they do so. Not only are mothers-in-law more likely to admit their faults in a disagreement, they are also about twice as likely to confront a problem head on. About ten percent of mothers-in-law are quick to tell their daughter-in-law when there is an offense between them while less than five percent of daughters-in-law will do so. And surprisingly about ten percent of mothers and daughters-in-law, at least sometimes, secretly wish their in-law were dead.

DAUGHTER-IN-LAW QUOTE: *When my in-law upsets me, I "try to forgive her."*

MOTHER-IN-LAW QUOTE: *When my in-law upsets me, I "can usually let it go and forgive her because she is an amazing woman."*

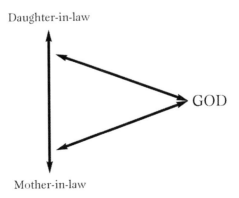

Unforgiving Janice

Therefore, as God's chosen people, holy and dearly loved, clothe yourselves with compassion, kindness, humility, gentleness and patience. Bear with each other and forgive whatever grievance you may have against one another. Forgive as the Lord forgave you (Colossians. 3:12-14, New International Version).

Daughter-in-law's Side

Janice and Mike just got back from a weekend at Mike's parents' home. As they lay in bed in the darkness of the night, Janice felt the bed softly shaking. She turned over to hear the sobs. She knew the tears were running down Mike's face onto his pillow.

She didn't even have to ask him what was wrong. Because of previous conversations following family visits, Janice pretty much knew he was thinking about this visit and probably about all the other ones she had made with him. She knew how much her drama, that usually started days before leaving, hurt him. The pattern was pretty much the same. Janice always dreaded the visit so much she would get physically sick to her stomach. She would resolve within herself not to say anything, but then self-doubt would overwhelm her and little comments here and there would emerge. Then, usually the day before the trip, the emotionally grand finale would arrive. It generally included hysterical screaming about things Janice believed Mike's mom thought about her; uncontrollable crying; and then, when she was physically drained, ended with resignation and embarrassment over her immature behavior. Withdrawn and sulking she would make the drive with Mike to his parents' house.

Janice couldn't begin to understand Mike's love for his mother, father, and sisters. There was something about Mike's relationship with his mother that always created havoc inside her. Janice always felt like she had a defect whenever she was around Betty. Betty was always offering to help Janice out, and somehow her kindness always made Janice feel like she couldn't measure up. Janice ended up feeling confused, frustrated, angry, and inadequate whenever she was around Mike's mom.

As she thought about her most recent reaction to Betty, coldness crept into Janice's heart. She decided to lie quietly beside Mike hoping they wouldn't have to go through that same old conversation about her behavior again. She was aware her pouting and curt responses made everyone uncomfortable at family gatherings. She also knew she should be proud of Mike, love him, and accept his family. She was tired of feeling insecure, tense, and guilty. At the center of her being, Janice shamefully felt like she would always be a disappointment to Mike. Janice believed she would never be able to measure up to Betty's standards.

Janice's childhood was so different from Mike's. Her parents drank almost every night. She calls them alcoholics. But if you asked them, they would tell you they don't have a drinking problem and could stop if they wanted to. Even though her parents were in church every Sunday to keep up appearances unless there was a big party the night before, they were always fighting. The screaming, hitting, and hateful words and looks her parents exchanged kept Janice frightened most of the time. She packed all that fear inside knowing she could never tell anybody what her life was really like.

After arriving at college, and really even in junior-high and high-school, she was for all practical purposes, on her own. Janice suspected her parents loved her. But she never knew her parents loved her like Mike knew his parents loved him. She really didn't have a clue what unconditional love meant. Janice was often ridiculed by her parents for embarrassing them in front of their friends. Neither of them knew how to show unconditional love. They were always either working or partying. They never seemed interested in spending time with Janice unless it was to chastise her. And so, hurt piled upon shame, and shame upon hurt and, somewhere along the way, Janice vowed never to allow herself to feel pain again. She slowly built a nearly impenetrable fortress around her heart. As much as she wanted to, she couldn't risk letting anyone in.

Mother-in-law's Side

Betty was aware Janice grew up with alcoholic parents. Though Janice never brought it up, friends who knew Janice's parents confided to Betty that Janice never even knew if there would be food on the table or even in the cabinets for that matter. Both Janice's parents had high profile jobs in their small community but began drinking in the early afternoon. Usually loud arguing followed until Janice was asleep. Betty knew Janice rarely received affirmation, encouragement, or even kind words from either parent.

Betty knew all that, but still she had a hard time dealing with Janice's behavior. Janice's pouting made it very clear to everyone in the family she didn't want to be around. And it made communication with Janice tense, stressful, and almost impossible. Betty and her husband, Curtis, always felt like they were walking on eggshells around Janice. They were constantly aware of the unpredictability and fragility of Janice's emotions. "I'm sure Janice acts that way because she never had the kind of love our family shows each other," Betty rationalized to Curtis to excuse Janice's rudeness.

Betty wants very much to love Janice like she loves her own children. But she knows Janice doesn't trust her intentions and won't allow Betty to get close. She also knows that if Janice had her way, she would never be allowed to see either Janice or Mike.

Betty feels bad for Mike because he doesn't have the freedom to invite her and Curtis over or to spend time with them unless he gets permission from Janice. And Mike doesn't approach Janice with the idea because he knows just mentioning it to her will create an argument.

Betty is constantly seeking ways to show Janice she really loves her. She wants Janice to know that she doesn't judge her for her past and that she cares deeply for her just as she is. Betty sees there can be a bright future for Janice and a better marriage for both Janice and Mike if Janice can put her past behind her and find the peace and freedom God offers.

God's Angle – Forgiveness versus Bitterness

Janice has never forgiven her parents for the emotional abandonment and ridicule they subjected her to during her growing-up years. And now her hardened heart affects her relationship with Mike and his family.

An unforgiving spirit produces bitterness which can become a stronghold. Noah Webster defines a stronghold as a fastness; a fort; a fortified place. The foundation of the fortress often built around the human heart is constructed with bitterness. Bitterness is often what happens when you choose to resolve a problem by not resolving it. If you are bitter and allow bitterness to continue, it will strengthen the fortress that encircles your heart. And as long as you maintain that fortress by nurturing the bitterness and refusing to forgive, you allow the person who hurt you to have emotional control over you.

Allowing past hurts to become your focus will keep you from breaking free from that stronghold. There's an old proverb that says an unforgiving spirit, when allowed to take root, is like taking poison and waiting for the other person to die. The past will always be with you – good or bad.

Author and pastor, Gary Inrig adds, "Forgiveness is free to the forgiven but costly to the forgiver, because the forgiver pays." Jesus paid His life for us in order that we might through faith (by His grace) forgive others. Through faith, confidence in Christ that He is who He says He is and has the power to do what He says He did and will do,

Janice can do all things – even forgive her parents. Through faith in Christ she can have the power to break the strongholds she began building as a child – strongholds that, if not destroyed, can be passed on to her children. Forgiveness is one of the hardest things to do. In Matthew 18: 21-35, Jesus instructs Peter, through the parable of the unmerciful servant, to forgive not seven times seven but seventy times seven.

And as a child of God you are commanded in Colossians 3: 1-17 to:
- Set your heart – your love - on things above.
- Set your mind – your thoughts - on things above.
- Put to death whatever belongs to the earthly nature.
- Put on the things from above-clothe yourselves with Christ's righteousness.

Colossians 3: 1-17 also allows you to see what has been ascribed to you as a child of God. You walked in earthly ways before trusting Christ. But once you trust Christ you are commanded to get rid of all those earthly ways that include: anger, rage, malice, slander, filthy language, and lying. You are to take them off like you would take off dirty clothes – piece by piece. Then you are to put on the new self – the self Christ gives to you when you place full confidence in Him to rescue you from your dirty destructive self and lead you in a better way – His way of living life. As a child of God, you are not called to air out, fluff, or even wash your old clothes and put them back on. Rather you are told to give up and reject your old clothes and live in the new clothes given to you through faith in Christ Jesus.

Putting on the new self begins when you are cleansed from the inside out by the work of Christ. It continues by the putting on of fresh clean clothes. The new clothes, given to you by Christ, are compassion; kindness; humility; gentleness; patience; and above all, love. And then, through the love Christ imparts to you, you are to bear with each other and forgive whatever grievances you may have against another just as the Lord forgave you.

This changing of clothes isn't easy and it doesn't happen overnight.

This taking off and putting on is a supernatural process controlled by God. But it requires your faith in Him and obedience to Him. You must remain focused on Christ's example and instruction for living. Ephesians 5: 18 encourages you *"not get drunk on wine, which leads to debauchery"* (wickedness). Instead you are to, *"be filled with the Spirit"* (New International Version). This filling of compassion, kindness, humility, gentleness, patience, and love is controlled by God and is continuous. It is a lifetime filling – not once in a lifetime but an everyday, moment-by-moment filling. The peace of Christ will began to rule in your hearts and whatever you do in word or deed you will desire to acknowledge God and all His Glory which means you will desire to affirm that God is all He says He is.

As you are filled or controlled by His Spirit – the product of this process will bring you to a thankful heart overflowing with joy because you know you have eternal life with Christ. Jesus said, the water I give will become a spring of water welling up to eternal life (John 4: 13). Take time to think about how knowing you have eternal life brings joy.

Where are You on the Triangle?
Reflect on your relationship with your in-law and honestly answer the following.

1. Do past hurts affect your relationship with your husband, children, in-law, or extended family? If so, how?

2. How would your conversation and behavior change if you stopped holding grudges?

3. How would your relationship with your in-law be different if the bitterness and grudges in your life disappeared?

4. Do you enjoy dwelling on past hurts and bitter feelings? Or is it your deep desire to rid yourself of strongholds built by bitterness?

5. Are you willing to trust God to remove all bitterness and replace it with His joy and thankfulness?

Finding God's Perspective

Use a Bible to help you answer the questions below.

1. As you seek God's perspective, ask Him to show you if a bitter unforgiving spirit has taken root in you. If it has, ask God to show you through His word how to conquer it.

    a. Mark 10: 27

    b. Matthew 6: 14-15

    c. Romans 8: 28-29

    d. Philippians 4: 8

    e. 1 John 1: 7-9

2. List the scriptures that spoke to you.

    a. Select and meditate on one for a month.

    b. Expand that list the following month to include a new scripture to encourage you to clothe yourself with God's righteousness.

Trust God to Make the Move

God's work is completed from the inside out. By giving God her old earthly thoughts, childhood memories, emotions, and behaviors and trusting Him to replace those earthly ways with His thoughts and ways, Janice's heart will be healed. Peace and thankfulness will begin to reign over her heart and mind. And as she purposes by His grace to walk in her new clothes, controlled by the Holy Spirit, God's true peace will begin to affect all Janice's relationships – including her relationship with her mother-in-law.

Try This:

1. As you began each day with a time of prayer and meditation, God promises to work on your behalf to change you. Your part is to trust Him and be obedient to His truth. Write down the bad memories and old clothes kind of thoughts you focus on. During your prayer time, ask God to take them from you and clothe you with His new way of thinking.

2. Memorize Philippians 4: 8. Each time your mind takes you back to the old earthly thought patterns, quote Philippians 4:8 out loud.

An Ending Thought

"Forgiven people will never really lay hold of the fullness of their forgiveness by God until they become forgiving toward others. Great forgivers inspire great love."

–Gary Inrig

NOTES

While about half of the mothers and daughters-in-law surveyed said they respect their in-law's different ways of doing things, about three-fourths said they complained about their in-law to others and criticized her decisions. At least half of these women believe their in-law also criticizes them.

But, on the positive side, almost all of the mothers and daughters-in-law said they pray about their attitudes toward their in-law and ask God to help them accept her.

DAUGHTER-IN-LAW QUOTE: *I wish my mother-in-law would, "be less critical."*

MOTHER-IN-LAW QUOTE: *I wish my daughter-in-law would "not be so critical."*

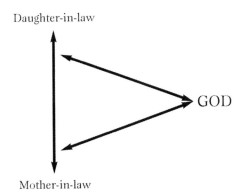

Complaining Carol

Do everything without complaining or arguing, so that you may become blameless and pure, children of God without fault in a crooked and depraved generation, in which you shine like stars in the universe (Philippians 2: 14-15, New International Version).

Daughter-in-law's Side

"I have to get out of this house. I'm so mad and depressed since I found out my mother-in-law is moving to Florida. Why does she think we moved away from Michigan? It was a way to get away from HER – that's why! It was never the climate, even though that was the reason we used for relocating. How could she do this to us? I could just scream. Ahhhhhh!"

Slipping into her newest shorts, the pair she definitely wouldn't wear around her mother-in-law, Carol climbed into her car, the one her mother-in-law, Sarah, thought was an extravagance, slammed the door, and sped toward the nail salon. Some of her friends would be there, and Carol needed to vent.

Carol bolted into the salon. "Uh oh! Here comes the drama," Beth whispered to Marcie who greeted Carol with a forced smile. "Hey Carol. What's up?" Beth asked. Immediately Carol felt better because now she would have a sympathetic audience. She began her tale of doom, despair, agony, and excessive misery.

"Hey, you'll never believe this one," Carol glared. "Of all people, guess who's moving here; MY MOTHER-IN-LAW – THE MEAN OLD WITCH - IN PERSON! We moved all the way to Florida just to get away from her meddling. I can't stand being around her. She tells me how to raise my children, how to keep my house, and any other thing she thinks about. I'll never have another happy day in this city." Then, from the *Wizard of Oz* soundtrack, she began singing, "Ding Dong! The Witch is dead. Which old Witch? The Wicked Witch! Ding Dong! The Wicked Witch is dead."

Somewhat shocked, Marcie and Beth didn't affirm most of Carol's reactions. Carol interpreted Marcie and Beth's silence as sympathy. With hesitation in a very soft voice, Beth added, "I actually really like my mother-in-law. She's pretty wonderful most of the time. I'll pray that your mother-in-law's move will work out better than you think."

A murmured and hesitant affirmation in Carol's voice could only be heard by a few people who had been listening to the conversation: "Thanks Beth. It will take a miracle for sure."

Mother-in-law's Side

Miles away in Michigan, Sarah was packing her bags, giving instructions to the movers, and thinking about how wonderful it was going to be to be near her family again and enjoy that wonderful Florida climate Carol was always bragging about. "I'll be so much help to Carol" thought Sarah. "It seems like she can never get organized. She's always complaining about how much she has to do every time I call. She's a wonderful mother, but the children seem to get on her nerves. So I'll try to help in any way I can."

"Carol, bless her, will be so grateful for my help," Sarah reassured herself. She quickly pushed aside the nagging thought, that maybe Carol wouldn't be so glad. "I love helping my family," Sarah rationalized. "Surely Carol will understand that. Since Jim passed away, my life has been so empty. My son seems to appreciate what I do for them. He's so much like his dad. Being around him makes me feel almost like Jim's still here."

In time, Carol will see how much help I'll be," Sarah consoled herself again. "It's really hard to move so far away from all my good friends. I'm getting older, and this move is difficult for me. But my family needs me. Not many mothers-in-law would make this sacrifice."

When the last box was loaded onto the van, Sarah took one last look, choked back a tear, and told herself that everything was going to work out fine when she arrived at her new Florida condo. She just knew her family would be so glad to see her.

God's Angle - Complaining

After Beth and Marcie left the salon, they decided to have lunch at a nearby tea room. Naturally their conversation was about Carol's "mother-in-law problem."

"I really feel for Carol. But, as usual, we're hearing only one side of the story," said Beth. "I told her I would be praying for her. And I am. I'm going to ask God to give Carol the grace she needs to react to her mother-in-law in a positive, Christian way. After all, she and her mother-law are both believers. Maybe Carol's mother-law doesn't realize that Carol resents her 'help' so much. Or maybe, once again, Carol is just blowing the whole thing out of proportion and complaining about nothing important."

"Yep, I think you're right Beth. I'll pray God will give us the wisdom and discernment we need to respond to Carol's complaints. I'm sure the topic will come up again. When I don't know what to do, I always try to remember God's promise in Jeremiah 33: 3, *'Call Me and I will answer you, and show you great and mighty things, which you do not know'* (New King James Version). During our Bible study time, let's take the time to search the Bible for direction.

Beth and Marcie are on the right track to helping their friend. God also can help you with a complaining in-law, or with your own complaints against your in-law, by supplying the necessary tools you need for solving your problems, and His advice is always best.

The Bible as a tool: God has something to say to you about complaining.

"Do everything without complaining or arguing" (Philippians 2: 14,

New International Version). This verse is worth repeating because it speaks to us individually.

"Friends, don't complain about each other. A far greater complaint could be lodged against you, you know. The Judge is standing just around the corner" (James 5: 9, The Message).

Prayer as a tool: You have something to say to God.

Ask God to create a clean heart in you (Psalm 51:10), to rid you of a complaining spirit, and to renew a steadfast spirit within you so you can do His will without grumbling (Philippians 2: 14). When you find yourself complaining about your in-law, know that God has ordained your days. The psalmist in Psalm 139:16 (New King James Version) declares to God, *"Your eyes saw me before I was put together. And all the days of my life were written in Your book before any of them came to be."*

Pray that God will show you your in-law obstacle is really an opportunity. Ask Him to show you what He wants YOU to learn from situations with your in-law that you tend to gripe about. Ask God how He wants YOU to change. Remember, God wants what is best for you, and sometimes allows trials, or people who cause them, in your life for the purpose of improving you. James 1: 2-4 (New King James Version) admonishes, *"My brethren, count it all joy when you fall into various trials, knowing that the testing of your faith produces patience. But let patience have its perfect work, that you may be perfect and complete, lacking nothing."* Ask Him for forgiveness and for the strength and wisdom to know how to deal with your in-law.

Thank God for your in-law and all the problems she brings to your life. 1 Peter 1: 6-7 (New Living Translation) encourages, *"So be truly glad. There is wonderful joy ahead, even though you have to endure many trials for a little while. These trials will show that your faith is genuine. It is being tested as fire tests and purifies gold—though your faith is far more precious than mere gold. So when your faith remains strong through many trials, it will bring you much praise and glory and honor on the day when Jesus Christ is revealed to the whole world."*

Pray that you will see the good in your in-law even if it's only a tiny bit. Ask God to reveal to you the love and goodwill in your in-law's heart. Then ask God to help you let your in-law live and kill the mean old witch image you have of her. Ask God to allow joy to come into your heart. As the Mayor of Munchkin City, in the County of the Land of Oz says, "Yes, let the joyous news be spread. The wicked Old Witch at last is dead!" You, and everyone around you, will be glad that horrible image of her is gone.

Christian Friends as a tool: God uses others to encourage and enlighten you.

1 Thessalonians 5: 11-12 (New International Version) says, *"Therefore encourage one another and build each other up, just as in fact you are doing. Now we ask you, brothers, to respect those who work hard among you, who are over you in the Lord and who admonish you."*

Where are You on the Triangle?
Reflect on your relationship with your in-law and honestly answer the following.
1. Who do you identify with most – Carol or Sarah?
2. What complaints do you have against your in-law?
3. What complaints might your in-law have against you?
4. How has your family been affected by your complaining attitude?

Finding God's Perspective
Use a Bible to help you answer the questions below.
1. Is there any way you can experience peace in spite of all the in-law problems that burden you?
   a. Philippians 4: 6-7
2. Do you wonder if the Lord has forgotten you?
   a. Psalm 13
3. You can always control your response to a conflict. How does complaining against your in-law help solve the problem or make you feel any differently about her?

       a. Proverbs 19:11

4. In any in-law relationship, there is always your side and her side. Examine yourself to see if there are changes you can make that will enable you to establish a better relationship with your in-law.

       a. Psalm 133: 1

       b. Psalm 139: 23-24

Trust God to Make the Move

Beth and Marcie did pray and search the Bible to see what God had to say about complaining. So the next time they saw Carol, they were ready to confront Carol's criticisms.

But instead of bombarding them with a tyrant of complaints against Sarah, Carol apologized to her friends for her earlier reaction to the news about her mother-in-law's move. She seemed really embarrassed about the witch song.

"I asked God to teach me how to solve this problem with Sarah," Carol said as she hung her head. And He did. He showed me verse after verse about how complaining is wrong, how he uses trials to change me, and how I should rejoice in the middle of my problem. He taught me to be thankful for Betty because, for one thing, I wouldn't have my husband if it weren't for her. And He reminded me that both of you were praying for me. Thanks for caring enough about me not to condone my wrong behavior. I admit I am still having problems dealing with Betty being so close to home. Please keep praying that I'll be able to respond to her in a loving way."

Try This:

Face it. People can be difficult, and it isn't likely that you can change them, but follow this plan, and think of it as "A" for effort:

1. ACCEPTANCE – Admit that your in-law was not made to please you. Recognize only God can change you and only God can change your in-law.

2. ACKNOWLEDGEMENT - Make a list of your in-law's good

qualities, and, if possible, let her know you recognize them.

3. ATTITUDE - Stop complaining about your in-law. Complaining won't change your in-law, but it will change you.

4. ANCHOR - Let God give you the stability, protection, and strength that will prevent you from drifting into the sea of regret.

An Ending Thought

Alfred, Lord Tennyson, *Idylls of the King*, penned these words said by King Arthur when he was dying: *"Pray for my soul. More things are wrought by prayer than this world dreams of."* How true.

Prayer

Forgive me Lord for having a complaining spirit. Help me turn my complaints over to You. Your word says You care for me. May your Holy Spirit guide me and teach me. I realize that I can't solve this situation without Your help. Give me peace. Thank You for Your love and understanding.

–Amen

Ninety percent of mothers and daughters-in-law surveyed said they would like for their relationship with each other to grow positively but only fifty percent of the mothers and daughters-in-law describe their relationship as above average.

When asked to complete the sentence, "I fear my in-law and I will never...," forty-four percent of mothers-in-law and sixty-eight percent of daughters-in-law expressed that they fear they may never have a close and loving relationship.

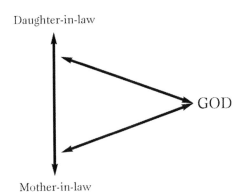

Aspiring Allison

Charm is deceptive, and beauty is fleeting; but a woman who fears the Lord is to be praised (Proverbs 31:30, New International Version).

Mother-in-law's Side

It was late spring. A gentle, cool, early evening breeze was blowing, and the guests were settling into the small, white, sea-side chapel for Allison and Jerry's wedding ceremony. Family portraits were being made at the front of the chapel. Joan, Allison's mother-in-law to be, was orchestrating the photo shoot for her side of the family.

Unless you knew them really well, you could hardly tell Jerry apart from his twin brother, Jim. Their relationship pretty much fit the identical-twin profile. They loved each other dearly. During their growing-up years, they shared almost everything – sports, friends, and leisure time.

Through the years, Joan had watched the boys grow with an increasing bond between them. They looked alike, thought alike, and now they would be sharing all their close ties and past memories long distance with Jerry's new wife. Joan wondered how the twins' relationship would be affected.

All in all, Joan's family was very warm and supportive. Joan and her husband, Rob, had pretty much centered their lives on the needs of the twins. These two parents had spent their last twenty-three years prayerfully and carefully preparing the boys intellectually and spiritually for the time they would meet the grown-up world on their own. On this day, that time had come for Jerry.

Joan felt good about Jerry and Allison's marriage, and her hopes were high that Allison was excited about becoming a part of Jerry's family. She and Rob wanted very much to surround Allison with that same love and warmth that flowed through their family.

Daughter-in-law's Side

Jerry and Allison had dreamed about, planned for, and waited, what seemed like forever, for this day during their last year of college. Emotions were running high and they both were anxious to get through the events of the day.

Allison never felt love before as strong as the love she felt for Jerry. She couldn't even imagine that she could spend her life with anyone else. Jerry was the perfect man for Allison and she could hardly wait to start her married life with him.

While Allison had no doubts that Jerry was the one for her, she wasn't so sure about spending the rest of her life with ties to his family. Allison, an only child, had grown up to be an independent thinker. A high priority for her parents was training Allison to be self-sufficient. Her parents were kind for the most part, but much more reserved and career-oriented than Jerry's family. Allison, who became a Christian during her sophomore year in college, really wants to be the kind of wife that God would approve of, but she can't understand the need to consult with the members of Jerry's family about every little decision.

Allison's insides churned at the thought of juggling relationships with Jerry's parents and brother the rest of her married life. To understand her mother-in-law to be, she tried to put herself in Joan's shoes. It was a stretch, but Allison tried to imagine giving away a son in marriage one day. She was sure she would want to have a good relationship with his wife. And she wanted to be a good daughter-in-law to Joan. Allison hoped she would be able to fit into Jerry's family. Her plan was to give it her best shot.

God's Angle –Virtuous Aspirations

Will Allison ever understand the love relationship Jerry's family has? Will she be jealous? Will Allison subconsciously be a wedge in the family's relationships? How will she handle the family gatherings? Will Joan be able to develop a compatible relationship with Allison? Will Joan be able to emotionally let Jerry go and be joined to Allison? How will Joan respond if Jerry takes the job he's been offered that will move him and Allison twelve hours away? Will Joan understand if Jerry and Allison spend Christmas with Allison's family?

These are the questions that nag at the minds of these two women who love and adore the same man. The answers hang on each woman's spiritual goal. In Joan and Allison's case, the goal is the same; they both desire to be godly Christian women.

Proverbs 31 describes the woman that both of these ladies aspire to be. This section of scripture describes virtues for women to imitate and for men to admire.

The Proverbs 31 woman carries significant responsibility both in her household and in the community. She is loved and admired by her husband and appreciated greatly by her children and employees. As the mother-in-law or daughter-in-law, the virtuous woman brings godly character to her dealings with all those she encounters - especially the fragile in-law relationship.

Examine the following scripture, to see a description of the virtuous woman from God's perspective. Note: All quotes in this section are from the New International Version

Her character is noble: Proverbs 31: 10, 30

"Charm is deceptive, and beauty is fleeting" (verse 30). Physical beauty by itself will eventually disappoint. But noble or virtuous character (verse 10) adorns a woman like jewels. Noble character is not the absence of social grace, which has limitations and is often misused. A woman of noble character is gracious, dignified, decent, good, and righteous at her core. This praiseworthy woman is

established on a more lasting foundation than charm and beauty.
Her husband and children praise and bless her: Proverbs 31: 11-12, 23, 28

Proverbs 12: 4 says, of a virtuous woman, *"A wife of noble character is her husband's crown, but a disgraceful wife is like decay in his bones."* *"Her husband has full confidence in his noble wife and lacks nothing of value"* (verse 11). *"She brings him good not harm all the days of her life"* (verse 12) and *"he is respected at the city gate"* (verse 23). *"Her children will arise and call her blessed; her husband also, and he praises her"* (verse 28).

Husbands have a part to play too. They are challenged to *"love their wife as Christ loved the church and gave himself up for her"* (Ephesians 5:25, New International Version). As men and women follow the biblical patterns God sets for them, it brings respect and a deep level of trust between them. They are both released to be the best they can for God and for each other.

She has no fear of the future (Proverbs 25, 30)

"She is clothed with strength and dignity; she laughs at the days to come" (verse 25). The most valuable garments godly women can wear are not made of silk and linen, but of godly virtues. Relinquishing yourself to fear the unknowns of the future is incompatible with a godly character since it exhibits a lack of confidence in the reality and sufficiency of your Heavenly Father. When you fear (worship and respect) God, your behavior drives out the fear of others, and you can see the thing He has planned for you more clearly. *"A woman who fears the Lord is to be praised"* (verse 30).

She works hard and opens her hands to the needy (Proverbs 13-14, 16b, 17, 18b, 20)

Read these verses on your own and notice the women described works energetically and is "on call" at night. She gives to the poor and helps the needy. These verses show a woman working hard not because she is intent on becoming wealthy, but because she wants to provide for her household and the disadvantaged around her. She sees herself as an instrument in God's hand for the good of others and His glory.

Where Are You on the Triangle?

Reflect on your relationship with your in-law and honestly answer the following.

1. How would your in-law describe your character?
2. What does your husband say about you? How do your children describe you?
3. Are you anxious about upcoming events? Do you worry about the future?
4. How do you spend your day?
5. The world wants you to believe it's all about you. Who do your daily activities benefit?

Finding God's Perspective

Use a Bible to help you answer the questions below.

1. Read Proverb 31: 10-31. Read it again in more than one version if possible.
2. From this passage, identify and list the qualities or virtues of this woman.
3. Ask God to show you the qualities that describe you. Circle them. What qualities do you have that are not described in these verses?
4. What value does this woman's husband attribute to her?
5. What quality of this woman do you admire most? Why?
6. Which qualities have you observed in your in-law?
7. What attributes would you like in your own life?

Trust God to Make the Move

Suppose Joan and Allison both move forward to a deeper relationship with God, do you think they can experience a relationship with each other free of great conflict? Remember, the virtuous woman *"speaks with wisdom, and faithful instruction is on her tongue"* (Proverbs 31:26, New International Version).

Allison and Joan are seeking God's heart. "Seek first the kingdom of God and His righteousness, and all these things shall be added to you" (Matthew 6:33, New King James Version). The Proverbs 31 woman is a model worth striving for. She is trustworthy, industrious, organized, and loving. As Allison and Joan increase in God's wisdom, with fear and reverence, relationships and priorities will become balanced.

Try This:

1. Ask God to give you a heart for Him and change you in any area He sees fit.
2. Memorize Proverbs 31:10-31
3. Choose one virtue from Proverbs 31: 10-31 that you want in your life. Describe how possessing that quality will affect your relationship with your in-law.

An Ending Thought

"Trust in the Lord with all your heart, and do not trust in your own understanding. Agree with Him in all your ways, and He will make your paths straight."

–Proverbs 3: 5-6 (New Life Version)

More than seventy-five percent of mothers and daughters-in-law surveyed said they usually offer to help when they see their in-law in need. However, more than twice as many daughters-in-law than mothers-in-law said they expect their in-law to help them given a moment's notice. Daughters-in-law are also two times more likely than mothers-in-law to drop by their in-law's home unannounced or on short notice.

DAUGHTER-IN-LAW QUOTE: *I expect my mother-in-law "to own up to her selfish and irresponsible ways."*

MOTHER-IN-LAW QUOTE: *I resent it most when my daughter-in-law "doesn't bother to thank anyone in our family for gifts."*

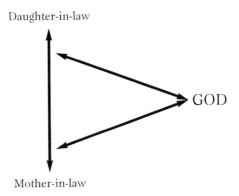

✳✳✳

Burdensome Britney

Give to everyone who asks you, and if anyone takes what belongs to you, do not demand it back (Luke 6: 30, Today's New International Version).

Mother-in-law's Side

"I'm beginning to think giving them grocery money and buying Isaac's baby clothes may be hurting more than helping. I only do it because of Isaac. I don't want to see that baby suffer. But Chris and I are barely making it. We're in our fifties and we have to start thinking about saving for our old age.

I've told my son, Wesley, he needs to get a second part-time job to help make ends meet; that's what his dad did when we needed money. And if all Britney is going to do is leave Isaac at the daycare all day so she can shop and hang out with her friends, she may as well get a job too. She doesn't have any kind of professional training but I know they're looking for a cashier in town at Everything Nice. If she worked there, at least she would be able to get a discount on all those new clothes she wants so badly.

I know Britney came from a dysfunctional family. Her mom is as irresponsible and as immature as Britney. When Britney's mom doesn't get her way, she just leaves home and goes on some ridiculously expensive trip she can't afford. I was floored the first time Britney did that until I learned her history. I know she feels rejected too. Her biological dad, who is very well-off financially, barely has anything to do with her. There is no one in Britney's family that will help.

I guess it's just my lot in life to help bear their financial burden but

I really would like to tell Britney and Wesley how much Chris and I have to sacrifice for them. Everyone says I should take up for myself. I just don't know what else to say. Chris agrees, but he doesn't offer any solutions."

Daughter-in-law's Side

"It's not fair. I deserve to have something new every now and then without getting the third degree about financial responsibility from Wesley's mom. Don't all newly married couples have to have help in the beginning? I don't know why June is always whining about helping us out. We have to eat!

June thinks I should get a job. But none of my friends work. They're still in college like I should be. I really want to be a teacher, but every time I start classes I have to drop out because between housework and taking care of Isaac, I don't have time to study. It's not my fault Central University won't give a full refund after the drop date. My friends have it made. They don't have to pick up after husbands, wash clothes, or worry about a house payment and grocery money. They have time to party and to study.

Nothing ever works out for me. How do I always get into these messes? I really hate depending on June and Chris because I'm tired of being lectured. But Wesley's parents are just going to have to suck it in and help us out until we can get on our feet."

God's Angle – Burdensome In-Laws

There are burdensome people of all ages. Some are Christians. Others are not. Mothers-in-law can be difficult. Daughters-in-law can be demanding. In some relationships, both in-laws are wearisome. Some in-laws mooch off your time while others devour your financial resources, or just like to use your stuff.

Bad things happen to everyone. Sometimes, even normally considerate and conscientious women must appeal for help because they are thrust into a tough situation. These urgent appeals for help are not the same as taking advantage of others, begging, robbing, or stealing. Scripture strongly admonishes you to care for fellow Christians in crisis. Titus 3: 14 (Today's New International Version) says, *"Our people must learn to devote themselves to doing what is good, in order to provide for urgent needs and not live unproductive lives."*

Genuinely burdensome people hassle you because it IS their character and typifies their lifestyle. These girls mooch because they are idle (lazy, unoccupied, at leisure) and are therefore unproductive and lack resources. Or they take advantage of you because they would rather use your belongings or time rather than their own. "Get lost!" "Grow up!" "Eat your own food!" "Do it yourself!" and "Get a job!" are expressions that come to mind when dealing with these women.

Wouldn't it be wonderful if the Bible supported your free-speech rights? It doesn't. But it does have guidelines for dealing with burdensome women. On one hand, scripture actually condemns the behavior of burdensome Christians, restricts dealings with them, and instructs fellow Christians to challenge these women to live productive lives. But on the other hand, when it comes to burdensome in-laws who are unbelievers, Christ calls His followers to a higher standard of behavior – a higher standard of loving, giving, letting go of, and forgiving.

Guidelines for Dealing with Burdensome In-Laws
I. Dealing with Burdensome Christian In-Laws
Read 2 Thessalonians 3: 6-15 and consider the guidelines below.
   A. Don't Be Burdensome Yourself
      Don't:
      - be idle.
      - eat another's food without paying for it.
      - be a burden to anyone.
      - be a busybody.
      - lead an undisciplined life.
      - tire of doing good.

Do:
- work hard.
- live an active and productive life.
- lead a settled and orderly life.

B.   Don't Enable Fellow Christians to Be Burdensome

Don't:
- associate with burdensome Christians so they will feel ashamed.
- consider burdensome Christians your enemies.

Do:
- identify through observation those who are habitually burdensome.
- warn fellow believers not to be idle.

When warning fellow believers remember to examine yourself first and then correct with love (John 8: 7, Matthew 7: 3-5, Proverbs 15: 1).

II. Dealing with Burdensome <u>Non-Christian</u> In-Laws

Read Luke 6: 27-36 and consider the guidelines below.

Do:
- consider them enemies.
- love ungrateful and unbearable people just as God loves them.
- bless them.
- allow them to take your stuff from you more than once.
- give them what they ask for more than once.
- show mercy.

Don't:
- expect or demand repayment.

Christ's love-your-enemy teaching makes it difficult to defend yourself against burdensome non-Christians. Actually, it is very hard to find scripture anywhere in the Bible that does direct you to protect yourself from them. Throughout the Bible though, verse after verse makes it clear that defense is something Christians should do, not for themselves but for those who are weaker. The poor, the needy, widows, and orphans are often given as examples. Jeremiah 22 and

Isaiah 1 are good illustrations of how God feels about those who oppress His people and how He expects His people to defend weaker ones. *"Learn to do right! Seek justice, encourage the oppressed. Defend the cause of the fatherless. Plead the case of the widow,"* God instructs Isaiah to tell the rulers (Isaiah 1: 17, Today's New International Version). God even says that to know Him means to defend, *"the cause of the poor and needy..."* (Jeremiah 22: 16, Today's New International Version).

If you are the one that needs defending, verse after verse says that God is your defender: Believing this is what it means to be meek. Don't give up on Him even when you are in the middle of problems with your in-law and it seems all is lost. Shadrach, Meshach, and Abednego relied on God to protect them even when they were about to be thrown into the fiery furnace; it is interesting that God did come through for them only after they were thrown into the middle of the heat (Daniel 3). Isaiah 51 and Jeremiah 51 lay out God's plan for defending His people who are in the middle of terrible oppression. After great suffering, His plan of salvation came to pass just as He said. For several reasons, including your own perfecting, God often allows you to go through a few trials before He steps in (1 Peter 5:10) either supernaturally, like he did for the guys in the fiery furnace, or through other people, like he did for the nation of Israel as documented in the prophecies of Isaiah and Jeremiah.

God often treats you like a mom would treat her daughter who is on the playground with a single toy. When another child walks up and seems interested in playing with the toy, the mom says, "Share," because she wants to instill values like selflessness into her child. But when the mom is ready to leave and the other kid refuses to give her own child back the toy, she steps in on behalf of her distressed child to redeem her possession. That is what God does for you. He expects you to share, even with your enemies, who very well may include your in-law. But when you, in right standing with Him, are exploited, He works on your behalf for your best interests.

Where are You on the Triangle?

Reflect on your relationship with your in-law and honestly answer
the following.

1. In what ways do you expect your in-law to help make your
   life convenient?

2. What do you do when your in-law is in a personal crisis?

Finding God's Perspective

Use a Bible to help you answer the questions below.

1. Why should you make every effort to live a productive life?
   a. Proverbs 31: 10-31
   b. 1 Thessalonians 2: 9

2. If you are burdensome, what effect might your behavior have
   on your in-law?
   a. Numbers 11: 10-15
   b. Luke 15: 11-32

3. If you are burdensome, what should you do?
   a. Ephesians 4: 28

4. What blessings result from generosity?
   a. Psalm 37: 21-26
   b. Psalm 112: 4
   c. Proverbs 11: 25
   d. 2 Corinthians 9: 6, 11

5. If your in-law is a widow and needs help, how should your
   family respond?
   a. 1 Timothy 5: 3-16.

6. Who should you defend?
   a. Psalm 82: 3

7. What else should be defended?
   a. Philippians 1: 7

8. Who should you depend on to defend you?
   a. Psalm 12: 5
   b. Isaiah 50: 34

Trust God to Make the Move

If your in-law is a Christian, then you and every other Christian in her life should be lovingly teaching her how to live an orderly and productive life. In June's case though, her biblical response to Britney, a non-Christian, is to set an example for Christian living through mercy and love. June's Christian lifestyle (words and actions) should be a pattern for godly living and a light that leads Britney to salvation (Philippians 2: 14-16).

After confessing her grumbling attitude and bringing all her concerns about Britney to Christ (Psalm 55: 2 and 1 Peter 5: 7), June asked Chris to join her in prayer. She bowed her head and prayed Psalm 119:154 from memory: *"Father, Defend my cause and redeem me; preserve my life according to your promise"* (Today's New International Version). And then she trusted God to do just that.

Try This:

1. Make a list of all the things your in-law has done to help make your life easier.

2. Make a list of all the things your in-law has done to make your life harder. Make another list of the things you have done to make your in-laws life difficult.

3. Bring your list before God. Thank Him for the things your in-law has done to help make your life easier. Ask Him to help you forgive your in-law for the things she has done to make your life harder. Ask Him to forgive you for the things you have done to make your in-law's life difficult.

An Ending Thought

"In everything I've done, I have demonstrated to you how necessary it is to work on behalf of the weak and not exploit them. You'll not likely go wrong here if you keep remembering that our Master said, 'You're far happier giving than getting.'"

–The Apostle Luke, Acts 20: 35 (The Message)

Sixty percent of daughters-in-law surveyed who describe their relationship with their mother-in-law as above average said their mother-in-law made them feel like a part of the family. On the other hand, daughters-in-law who describe their relationship with their mother-in-law as below average said they feel like an outsider. It is interesting that, according to the survey, one-hundred percent of mothers-in-law perceive they treat their daughter-in-law like a loved family member.

DAUGHTER-IN-LAW QUOTE: *I wish my in-law would "accept me more as a daughter and not just a girl who married her son."*

MOTHER-IN-LAW QUOTE: *I wish my in-law would "treat me like she treats her family."*

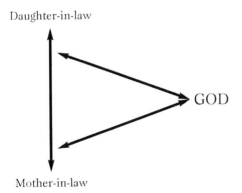

Intolerant Tess

You are all sons of God through faith in Christ Jesus, for all of you who were baptized into Christ have clothed yourself with Christ. There is neither Jew nor Greek, slave nor free, male nor female, for you are all one in Christ Jesus (Galatians 3: 26-27, New International Version).

Daughter-in-law's Side

"I was warned by my Jewish friends that John's family would never accept me as a loving member of the family but I was willing to compromise if it meant living peacefully with my in-laws. Being young and in love, nothing seemed impossible to me.

My parents were extremely disappointed in my decision to marry John because they were devout Jews, and they wanted their grandchildren to be brought up in the Jewish faith. I didn't understand how John's Christian background could present a difficulty. John wasn't attending church so I was sure that when the time came, I would be able to choose the religious faith of our children without a problem. But, I was forgetting about something. Church is very important to John's parents. They believe Jesus is God's son!

Unfortunately, my parents were right to be concerned. While John's religious background wasn't a problem with John, it has been a problem with my in-laws, especially my mother-in-law. I don't think I will ever be accepted by her, and frankly, at this point, I really don't care. My mother-in-law, Tess, has done nothing but criticize my religion. She is so intolerant of my beliefs. She insists our boys, Daniel and Eli, go with her to church even though I always take them to the synagogue every Saturday. I'm sure she probably talks about me behind my back. The boys tell me, when they are with her, she whispers with her friends all the time.

I am really turned off by Tess AND her Jesus. She is sooo judgmental and such a 'goody-goody.' At least I don't look down my nose at everyone who isn't Jewish. I don't go around her unless I just can't avoid it. No wonder church is such a bummer for John. At least, he doesn't mind if the boys and I attend services at the synagogue. And he seems to enjoy participating in Jewish holidays with my family. He knows his parents are prejudiced, but there's nothing he can do about it. I just wish I had been accepted by his family for who I am. That would have meant so much to me"

Mother-in-law's Side

"Well, The Good Book says that God won't put more on me than I can bear, so I will just have to bear my cross, and do the best I can. Ruth, my daughter-in-law, is such a burden on my heart. I thought when John married her she would change and see what a joy it is to be in a Christian family. For some reason, she won't even visit our church. Lord knows, I've tried to show her how wrong her beliefs are and yet she just can't seem to see the light. However, I'll see to it that Daniel and Eli know Jesus.

I'll have to admit that I really haven't been able to accept Ruth. She is so different. And those holidays she insists that the grandchildren celebrate are mind-boggling. I can't even pronounce the names—shan-kipper or something. And who can keep up with all those feasts? You'd think they would just have a few pot-luck dinners and be done with it.

Once, Ruth had the nerve to ask me why John didn't attend my church. Well, he probably would go if he wasn't afraid she would gripe about it. He knows how strong-willed she can be. All Jewish people are so stubborn. Life can sure get complicated. Sometimes it's just better to keep quiet—but is that witnessing?"

God's Angle - Prejudice

Then Peter began to speak: I now realize how true it is that God does not show favoritism, but accepts men from every nation who fear Him and do what is right" (Acts 10: 34, New International Version).

Ever since time began, some are always disappointed with their in-laws. In the first book of the Bible, Genesis 26: 34-35, we read about Esau, the son of Isaac and Rebekah, who actually married two Hittite (pagan) women. *"They were a source of grief to Isaac and Rebekah"* (New Living Translation). Later, in Genesis 27: 46, Rebekah said to her husband Isaac, *"I am weary of my life,"* (New King James Version) because of Esau's wives. On the other hand, in the book of Ruth, Naomi had a wonderful relationship with her daughter-in-law who was of another race.

What happens in the lives of some in-laws that reap happiness, and others who live in misery? Much depends on the way they accept others. Tess, for example, has never accepted her daughter-in-law; she is also self-righteous, prejudiced, and very opinionated.

Jesus teaches us by example. He was good to the Samaritan woman. Samaritans were not accepted in those days by Jews because Samaritans had inter-married. They were half-Jews and Jewish people did not associate with them (John 4: 9). Jesus was good to the tax collectors like Zacchaeus. They were hated by everyone (Luke 19: 5). Jesus healed people of other races. For example, He healed a Canaanite woman's daughter (Matthew 15: 21-28).

Jesus teaches us to accept one another: *"Accept one another, then just as Christ accepted you, in order to bring praise to God"* (Romans 15: 7, New International Version). You can't expect love and commitment unless you follow Jesus' example.

Where are You on the Triangle?

Reflect on your relationship with your in-law and honestly answer the following.

1. If your in-law comes from a different background, culture,

race, socio-economic status, or religious affiliation, do you let prejudice affect your relationship with her?

2. Reflect on the things you say about your in-law. Do your comments condemn or commend?
3. Are you a witness for Jesus or against Him?
4. Are you "too good" to see the best in your in-law?
5. Based on Jesus' examples above, what would He want you to do?

Finding God's Perspective
Use a Bible to help you answer the questions below.
What does "The Good Book" say to you?
1. Who is included in God's plan for salvation?
   a. John 3:16?
2. What teaching did the apostle Peter learn that we need to accept in our world today?
   a. Acts 10: 34
3. What should our attitude be?
   a. Philippians 2: 1-5
4. What advice does James give to us?
   a. James 2: 8-10
5. Is it possible to apply this verse to your in-law?
   a. Matthew 7: 12

Trust God to Make the Move
Before Tess and Ruth can have a good relationship, and before Tess can even think about introducing Ruth to Jesus, Tess has to change. Thank God, all things are possible with Him (Matthew 19: 26) because Tess has a lot of damage to overcome. She will have to recognize her own sin, ask God and Ruth to forgive her, and spend time learning about Ruth. After all that, she will have to ask God to show her how to be a witness for Him to Ruth, instead of a witness against Him.

Try This:

It is true that God works in mysterious ways. We don't always understand His methods. If you identify with Ruth, you probably feel resentment and most likely you feel turned off by your in-law's hypocrisy and racial prejudice. Jesus understands what you're going through. He was rejected and almost killed by people in His hometown because He was God's son (Luke 4: 16-30). But we are instructed to live peaceably with others as much as possible (Romans 12: 18). Try doing something special for your in-law (Psalm 34: 14). Goodwill, love, and faithfulness follow those who do good (Proverbs 11: 27, Proverbs 14: 22). God will convict your in-law through your kindness (Romans 12: 20).

If you identify with Tess, pray that God will show you how to reach out to your in-law. Toss out your judgmental attitude. Luke 6: 37-38 (The Message) says, *"Don't pick on people, jump on their failures, criticize their faults— unless, of course, you want the same treatment. Don't condemn those who are down; that hardness can boomerang. Be easy on people; you'll find life a lot easier..."* Learn about her. Understand her beliefs and customs. Do what Jesus did. Use them as a means to connect your in-law to Jesus. Jesus always understood the cultural backgrounds and beliefs of people He was trying to reach and teach. Remember the Samaritan woman and Zacchaeus, not to mention the scribes, Pharisees, and Sadducees. All His parables are also a good example of how He integrated culture into His teaching.

Also, realize how your attitude affects other family members who may feel forsaken by you and your in-law. Love can go a long way in dissolving problems in relationships. 1 Peter 4: 8 (New International Version) says, *"Above all, love each other deeply, because love covers over a multitude of sins".* No one is perfect. *"For everyone has sinned; we all fall short of God's glorious standard,"* (Romans 3: 23, New Living Translation). We can only trust God to guide us through this life and accomplish His will by teaching us how to love. *"But God showed his great love for us by sending Christ to die for us while we were still sinners"*

(Romans 5: 8, New Living Translation). Define love in this way:

Listen

Overlook faults

Value others

Express love

An Ending Thought

"If you judge people, you have no time to love them."

–Mother Theresa

Prayer

Heavenly Father, forgive me when I am judgmental and fail to love the ones in my life who may need love the most.

Amen

Mothers and daughters-in-law surveyed, at least sometimes, felt equally intimidated by the other in-law's relationship with their son/husband. But twice as many daughters-in-law felt threatened by changes in holiday plans.

DAUGHTER-IN-LAW QUOTE: *I wish my mother-in-law would, "be more sensitive and bend a little for others."*

MOTHER-IN-LAW QUOTE: *The thing that causes the most problems between my daughter-in-law and me is, "her control in most situations."*

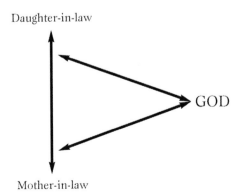

Jealous Judy

You are still worldly. For since there is jealously and quarreling among you, are you not worldly? (1 Corinthians 3:3, New International Version).

Mother-in-law's Side

As a single mom, Elizabeth took care of her two children alone. She was the one who got them up for school each morning, took them to all their after-school activities, and worked full time to provide for them. Her children were her life, and overwhelmed by activities, that centered on them and work, she had very little time for anything else.

Though she wanted to go to church because she believed it would be best for her children, most Sundays she was too exhausted to get there. One day a friend told Elizabeth about a speaker that would be at church the following week and invited her to come hear him. And so, that next Sunday Elizabeth made the extra effort to get up and go to church. She was glad she did. The speaker's message was a turning point in her life.

That fall day, the foundation of the message was Proverbs 3: 5-6: *"Trust in the Lord with all your heart and lean not on your own understanding; in all your ways submit to him, and he will make your paths straight* (Today's New International Version). Direction was just what she needed - direction in her life that would bring order to her home.

Elizabeth began to base her life on that verse. And as time passed, Elizabeth grew to trust God for everything – money to pay bills and food for the table. She even relied on God for energy and time to spend with her children after long work days. Just a night of popcorn and a rental movie became special. The children loved and adored their mother for giving herself so completely to them. Yes, there were times they couldn't understand why they weren't allowed to be part of activities other children were. But they knew God helped them through all those times and they grew up to become God-fearing adults.

Because Elizabeth had experienced a broken marriage she often prayed for future mates for her children. So, she could not have been more excited at the announcement of her son Jack's engagement to Judy since even before the engagement announcement was made Judy and Elizabeth already had a unique relationship; they were prayer partners and had shared in many long spiritual conversations. From Elizabeth's perspective, it seemed their relationship was built on mutual love and respect.

But the minute the engagement ring was placed on Judy's finger, the nice, sweet, kind, and gentle friendship she and Elizabeth had experienced suddenly ended. Judy began to pull away from Elizabeth and an adversarial spirit emerged. Judy's rejection crushed Elizabeth.

But Elizabeth's faith in God was strong and so she purposed to trust God with all the hurt she had experienced before the wedding and determined to overlook offenses in order to maintain a good relationship with Judy – a relationship that would honor God. She believed when the stress from the wedding, new jobs, and setting up home passed, things would get back to normal. But that didn't happen. Instead, as time passed, Elizabeth's relationship with Judy grew even more difficult.

After Elizabeth's grandchildren were born, Judy controlled Elizabeth's time with them. Judy told Elizabeth specific dates and times she could visit. Elizabeth was never allowed to be with her grandchildren alone. She was never permitted to take them on an outing to the toy store or the zoo. Judy wouldn't even let Elizabeth choose gifts for them.

Judy also controlled Elizabeth's contact with Jack. If Elizabeth called her son at home, it was always a three-way conversation. It was never Elizabeth's desire to be underfoot with Jack and Judy. Even if that had been true, it would have been impossible anyway because Elizabeth lived nine hours away. All Elizabeth really wanted was to love on Jack and Judy and spend some time with her grandchildren as they grew up.

Elizabeth often wondered what she had done to offend Judy. To Elizabeth, Judy's attitude seemed to scream, "Leave us alone! Get out of our lives!" For Elizabeth, it was extremely heart wrenching not to be able to see her family. To her, Judy seemed happiest when she had Jack and the children all to herself. All Elizabeth knew to do was to trust God for restoration, to trust Him to *"restore what the locust have eaten"* (Joel 2:25, New International Version).

One day Elizabeth finally found the courage to ask Judy about the conflict between them that had grown into a monster.

Daughter-in-law's Side

"I'm a private person and I don't have time for a relationship with my mother-in-law," Judy explained to her friend Beth one day during a discussion about their mothers-in-law. "She would spend way too much time with us if I didn't keep her at an arm's length. She wants to smother us. Anyway, I don't think I should have to interrupt my family's schedule or change my plans to accommodate her. And I definitely don't want any input from Elizabeth about the way it was when Jack was growing up. Just knowing how much Jack loves Elizabeth makes me feel like an outsider. The thought of being around her makes me sick inside. When I think about having to be with her, I never know what I will say or do."

Later that night Judy rehearsed the conversation she had with Beth and somehow she just didn't feel right about some of the things she said. "What's the problem?" she wondered. "I don't like feeling like this. I feel all ugly inside. How can I get peace in my relationship with Elizabeth? Am I jealous? Do I have a hard time relating to her because of my parents? They are so hard to get along with. Do I expect Elizabeth to treat me the same way? All I know is that being near Elizabeth upsets me. I can't handle it. It's just better for everybody if we stay apart."

God's Angle – Guilt, Fear, and Jealousy

If peace of mind could be bought, many people would give great sums of money. The peace of mind that Judy seeks is characterized by an absence of guilt, fear, and envy (jealousy). This peace is rarely found except in those who have learned to trust God. Once you come to know Jesus Christ as your personal Savior and Lord, you have, as the Apostle Paul puts it, *"peace with God, through our Lord Jesus Christ"* (Romans 5:1, New International Version).

As you come into a trusting relationship with God, it then becomes possible to have peace with yourself and with others. Jesus said, *"Peace, I leave with you; my peace I give unto you"* (John 14:27, New International Version). Judy will have to answer this question, "Is Christ really the center of my life and am I seeking first the kingdom of God and His righteousness?" (Matthew 6: 33).

Judy's attitude and behavior toward Elizabeth is rooted in jealousy, fear, and guilt. These three things are eating her up inside. And they will affect your relationship with your in-law. These three emotions are great enemies of a peaceful mind.

Guilt

In-laws with a guilty conscience are in a constant state of uncertainty and nervousness. They depend on their own wisdom and power to get through each day (Proverbs 28: 1). Even Christian in-laws often continue to suffer from past confessed sin because they fail to understand God has truly put their sins behind His back (Isaiah 38: 7). Once forgiven, God removes sins as far from you as the east is from the west (Psalm 38: 17). If you feel guilty because of past wrongs, seek the Lord and ask Him to forgive you for refusing to accept the reality of His mercy and grace. As you resolve by His power to put and leave those sins at the feet of Christ - those sins Christ has already taken punishment for - God will work in you. Peace will reign in you. Victory over turmoil will begin to be yours.

Fear

Chronic fear, from small or vague uneasiness to true anxiety, is harmful and can result in physical illness. This kind of fear is the result of not seeing your circumstances from God's perspective and trusting Him to do what is best for you. You may fear loosing material possessions, health, jobs, status, and loved ones. Or your fears may revolve around intimacy, rejection, condemnation, and even intrusion into your personal life. All these real and tormenting fears are destructive and will rob you of your peace of mind. To deal with fear, call upon the Lord. The psalmist says, *"I sought the Lord, and He answered me; He delivered me from all my fears"* (Psalm 34: 4, New International Version).

Jealousy

A heart of peace gives life to the body, but envy (jealousy) rots your bones (Proverbs 14: 30). When you take your eyes off what is important and place them on what is less important - when you fail to give your relationship with God top priority - it is easy for envy or jealousy to enter your heart and rob you of peace and contentment. But if you think more and more about God's love, promises, and commands for living life with others and less about selfish temporary things, your heart will began to change. Your thought patterns and focus will be more and more on God. A heart of peace will bring new life to your spirit.

Where are You on the Triangle?

Reflect on your relationship with your in-law and honestly answer the following.

1. Are you struggling with fear, guilt, or jealousy? Are any of these emotions affecting your relationship with your in-law?

2. When you try to determine what is wrong in your in-law relationship, do you primarily focus on your relationship with

your in-law or do you focus more on your relationship with God?

3. Do you value your time, opinions, personal way of doing things, appearance, status, or where you live more than your relationship with the Lord? Remember, *"a woman who fears the Lord is to be praised"* (Proverbs 31: 30b, New International Version).

Finding God's Perspective
Use a Bible to help you answer the questions below.

1. How does God view jealousy in the in-law relationship?
   a. Galatians 5: 19-26
   b. 1 Corinthians 3: 1-3
2. If you have a negative relationship with your in-law because of jealousy towards you and you have a right relationship with God, what should your response be?
   a. 1 Peter 4: 13
3. When is it okay to be jealous?
   a. 2 Corinthians 11: 2

Trust God to Make the Move

God's word gives instruction that can be applied to both sides of the in-law triangle. *"If you love those who love you, what credit is that to you? Even sinners love those who love them. And if you do good to those who are good to you, what credit is that to you? Even sinners do that....But love your enemies, do good to them and lend to them without expecting to get any thing back. Be merciful, just as your Father in heaven is merciful"* (Luke 6:32-36, New International Version).

On the day Elizabeth found the courage to approach Judy, God gave Elizabeth the words to say. With Luke 6: 32-36 fixed in her mind, she wrote Judy a letter. In the letter Elizabeth affirmed Judy, stated her decision of love for Judy, and asked Judy to forgive her for any attitude or action that had offended her. From that day on, Elizabeth consistently applied Luke 6:32-36 to all of her thoughts and actions toward Judy even when she was tempted not to. And as God opened doors, Elizabeth really did begin to love Judy unconditionally. Eventually, Judy softened toward Elizabeth and began to communicate with her through Jack. Much time has passed, but, amazingly, now Judy is the one who is pursuing time with Elizabeth. Surprisingly, on her own initiative, Judy just invited Elizabeth to spend Christmas with her, Jack, and the grandchildren – now teenagers.

What a blessing to see the move of both women toward God and toward each other. As you deal with jealousy, guilt, and fear are you willing to trust God's way?

Try This:

1. Ask God to give you a real longing to follow His way in solving conflict with your in-law.

2. Ask God to teach you what He has to say about guilt, fear, and jealousy. Ask Him to show you any guilty, fearful, or jealous motives that live in your own heart that fuel bad behaviors toward your in-law.

3. Pray like Jesus prayed, *"Lord not my will but Yours be done"* (Luke 22: 42b, New International Version).

4. Romans 6: 19 (New International Version) says, *"I put this in human terms because you are weak in your natural selves. Just as you used to offer the parts of your body in slavery to impurity and to ever-increasing wickedness, so now offer them in slavery to righteousness leading to holiness"*. Focus on these two thoughts, "I will no longer offer my mind and body to guilt, fear, and jealousy (impure thinking) that leads me to become wicked. Instead, I will offer my mind and body to right living that leads me to become holy".

An Ending Thought

"The jealous are troublesome to others, but a torment to themselves."
–English Quaker Leader and Founder of Pennsylvania, William Penn

All mothers-in-law surveyed said they never give unwanted advice, but daughters-in-law disagree. Almost half said their mother-in-law gives unsolicited advice. Only one-fifth of daughters-in-law surveyed said they had actually ever asked their mother-in-law for her opinion.

DAUGHTER-IN-LAW QUOTE: *I wish my in-law would "not be so opinionated."*

MOTHER-IN-LAW QUOTE: *When I pray about my in-law, I usually ask God "to make sure my mouth is closed."*

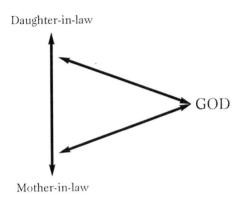

Independent Ulyssa

But they did not listen or pay attention; instead, they followed the stubborn inclinations of their evil hearts. They went backward and not forward (Jeremiah 7: 24, Today's New International Version).

Daughter-in-law's Side

"I wish she would just butt out! Every single time Leo and I try to make any kind of decision, she freaks out if it doesn't go her way. All she ever thinks about is what everybody will say. She likes to brag to her friends about our accomplishments – you know, our education, our jobs, where we live – stuff like that. She really doesn't care about me or about what's important to us as a couple.

Here's the latest example of her interference. Last week Leo was offered a new job. Taking the job will mean he'll make quite a bit less money. But it's a job that will allow Leo to feel like he's making a difference in the world and it will give him time to work on that novel he's been dreaming about writing. And those things are important to him - and me. Leo is so tired of sitting at a desk all day pushing around useless papers. And I really would like the adventure of a new place even if it does mean moving to a new city and pretty much eliminating my ability to shop.

Of course when Marissa, Leo's mom, found out we were considering making the move, she started her mud-slinging campaign. She should be a political strategist! Within an hour, her 'spin' was heard around the world.

Among all the cursing and threats of the entire family's eminent death because of worry over us, she basically called Leo stupid, selfish, and irresponsible. And we haven't even finished working through the decision-making process yet! I'm so tired of all her manipulation. She makes me so angry; I'm ready for Leo to make the decision to change jobs just to watch her squirm.

But, you know, I really don't think I should let my anger toward Marissa push Leo and me into doing something foolish. I really want to hear what God wants us to do."

Mother-In-Law's Side

"I remember when I was a young mom and wife like Ilyssa. I wouldn't listen to anyone – especially my mother-in-law. It was almost like going through my teen-age years again. Now that I think about it, my relationship with my mother-in-law was an all out rebellion. I didn't want to hear a thing she had to say – especially child-care advice. I found all the mistakes she made with Chip, my husband, and blamed her for all his less than desirable traits. I picked apart her conversations to find things I could use to build my case against her as an irresponsible mom. I'm sure it looked to all my friends like I hated her – and I think because of Chip's infantile behavior, hate and disgust probably were my main emotions towards her.

I don't want my daughter-in-law to have those feelings about me. I really want Ilyssa to like me, and so I really try hard to look out for her. I'm not sure Leo was really ready for the responsibility of marriage. Even though I think I've done a pretty good job raising a conscientious young man, he's still immature in some ways and can occasionally come up with some pretty foolish ideas like quitting his great job and, of all things, writing a novel. I really had to come down pretty hard on him about this latest silly idea. Quitting his job to become a non-profit manager for a start-up ministry – how stupid can he be? The company he works for now is established and has great benefits. I don't know what he thinks he'll do about health insurance or even grocery money for that matter. And if Leo wants to benefit society, why doesn't he go and volunteer at the local soup kitchen or something like that on the weekends? I'm sure if he looks hard enough surely he can find someone in his community to help. If he does quit, he'll be looking for people to help him! And I can just see me explaining that to all my friends.

Ilyssa must really be glad I'm still around to straighten him out so she doesn't have to. I'm sure she's grateful for my input. She has to know I have her best interests at heart.

When my own mother-in-law died, I know this is horrible to say, but I really felt a kind of relief. I knew without her around, I could straighten Chip out and get him to finally grow up. Now, I'm pretty ashamed of the way I felt and have lots of regrets because of the way I treated her when she was alive. I wished I had shown her more love and understanding. And I'm really sorry Leo didn't get to know her.

You know, even though I didn't approve of my mother-in-law's parenting skills, I really did want her to admire me. And other than his occasional off-the-wall ideas, I hope she would have liked the way I single-handedly raised Leo. And most of all, I hope she would have approved of the way I shaped up Chip to become a respectable husband and father.

Thinking back, you know, my mother-in-law had to have known I didn't respect her. It must have been very painful for her to love and raise a son and then watch him go off to, what probably seemed to her like, an enemy camp. Even though I was forced to be the way I was because of Chip's immaturity, I know I wouldn't want a daughter-in-law like me. I'm very fortunate - Ilyssa is not like me at all. She doesn't have to be. She can count on me to keep Leo straightened out."

God's Angle – Independent Attitudes

Even though the general perception is that mothers-in-law give unwanted opinions to daughters-in-law, the opposite is also true. Both in-laws are guilty of letting the smugness of self-sufficiency get in the way of really listening. When you're tempted to discard your in-law's words, try to put your right to independence aside for a few moments and consider these guidelines.

*Rummage through the garbage to find true wisdom. Don't let pride get in the way of finding wise words. God used a donkey to get the prophet Balaam's attention (Numbers 22). It is possible he could be using your in-law to get yours. So examine the bits of heavenly truth found in your in-law's annoying advice and unsolicited opinions and ignore the rest. The famous English biologist, Thomas H. Huxley, voices that idea this way: *"There is no greater mistake than the hasty conclusion that opinions are worthless because they are badly argued."*

King David exemplified this concept as he was fleeing the rebellion of his son, Absalom. As he made his way through the town of Bahurim, a man named Shimei came alongside him and begin cursing, throwing stones, and kicking dirt at him. As he continued down the road, Shimei walked alongside the ridge of a hill above David and added shouts of insults and horrible accusations to his already bad behavior. Shimei ended his frenzy with, *"And good riddance, you pathetic old man!"* (2 Samuel 16: 8, The Message).

The mighty men traveling along with King David were so angry; they wanted to cut Shimei's head off. Disagreeing, King David replied, *"Don't bother with him; let him curse; he's preaching God's word to me. And who knows, maybe God will see the trouble I'm in today and exchange the curses for something good"* (2 Samuel 16: 12, The Message). It's interesting that David could overlook the stones, dirt, curses, and insults being hurled at him and actually look for God's message and God's blessing through the words of this angry man. David was wise and his story ends well. Soon, he reached the river where he rested and was revived. Shimei apologized. David forgave. And shortly he got his kingdom back.

*Base your decisions on heavenly wisdom. Don't make decisions based on a defiant and prideful attitude. "I'll just show her!" will most likely result in bad outcomes for everyone involved. It is an unwise attitude because it delays progress. The Hebrew nation wandered in the wilderness and an entire generation of them never got to their destination because of that same attitude. Hebrews 3 is a synopsis of their story. *"For who were the people who turned a deaf ear? Weren't they the very ones Moses led out of Egypt? And who was God provoked with for forty years? Wasn't it those who turned a deaf ear and ended up corpses in the wilderness? And when he swore that they'd never get where they were going, wasn't he talking to the ones who turned a deaf ear? They never got there because they never listened, never believed"* (Verses 15-19, The Message).

Remember heavenly wisdom can be found in women of all ages. So don't arrogantly ignore advice and opinions from your in-law because she comes from a different generation than you. Just because your in-law is younger, don't discount her words. Many notable young women are found throughout the Bible. Esther risked her life to save her people. Mary was called favorable by the angel Gabriel and became the mother of Jesus Christ. Miriam rescued Moses and as a result, her nation escaped slavery. Ruth was called a woman of excellence. The evangelist, Phillip, had virgin daughters gifted with divine counsel. Thankfully, many godly young women are alive and well in today's world. God Himself said, in the last days, young women will give divine counsel (Acts 2: 17).

And just because your in-law is older and may not be aware of the latest child-rearing theories, doesn't mean she doesn't have wisdom to offer. In fact, older godly women are actually commanded in scripture to give advice to younger women. Titus 2: 4-5 advises older women, who don't gossip or drink too much, to give good counsel and be teachers of what is right and noble so they can teach younger women to be self-controlled, pure, busy at home, kind, subject to their husbands, and to love their husbands and children. Whoa! That covers lots of touchy subjects.

Listen to your in-law with an attitude of respect. A friend, whose relationship with her mother-in-law was based on mutual respect, had this insight: "What I experienced with Ann (I don't even like the word mother-in-law because it has such a negative reputation) was that she made me feel like I was a joy to her. And I considered her my greatest mentor. She was truly sent to me from God and part of the package was a wonderful husband."

Of course it's wonderful when there is mutual respect. But if that's not possible because your in-law is not agreeable, as difficult as it may be, remember, don't throw out God's message to you along with the curses and insults.

*Make sure the advice and opinions you GET and GIVE focus attention towards God and are based on godly principles. Or, if there is no biblical command, insure they come from a trustworthy godly source. Shimei wasn't behaving in a godly or trustworthy way, but David did consider the idea that God's counsel might be found somewhere in his words. On the other hand, the apostle Paul, when giving an answer about a subject God had not specifically addressed, said, *"I give my opinion and advice as one who by the Lord's mercy is rendered trustworthy and faithful"* (1 Corinthians 7: 25, Amplified Bible).

Also examine the motivation of the advice and opinions you're given. Are they words of truth, or are they just flattering words intended to win your friendship? Sometimes harsh words can be a message God uses to get your attention, can be meant for your good, or they can just be plain mean. Ask God for discernment and then go to the Bible to see if the words you hear agree.

Where are You on the Triangle?
Reflect on your relationship with your in-law and honestly answer the following.

1. When your in-law offers her opinion or advice, what is your general response?
2. What pervasive attitude underlies your responses?
3. When you give corrective or instructive advice or unsolicited opinions to your in-law, what source is your advice or opinion

based on? What motivation is your advice or opinion usually based on? If you're not sure, ask God to reveal it to you.

4. What tone do you use when giving advice or opinions to your in-law?

Finding God's Perspective
Use a Bible to help you answer the questions below.

1. What source should you rely on for counsel?
    a. Job 12: 13
    b. Psalm 32: 8
2. What advice should be ignored?
    a. Proverbs 3: 5-7
    b. Ezekiel 13: 17-23
    c. 2 Timothy 2: 16
3. What is the purpose of counsel?
    a. Proverbs 1: 5
    b. Proverbs 19: 20
    c. Proverbs 23: 19
4. How can you recognize wise godly counsel?
    a. Proverbs 13: 16
    b. Proverbs 14: 1, 29
    c. Proverbs 28: 26
5. What happens when godly counsel is ignored?
    a. Psalm 81: 11-12
    b. Jeremiah 6: 19
    c. Zechariah 7:13
    d. Luke 6: 49
6. What emotional responses does God have when His counsel is ignored?
    a. Jeremiah 13: 17
    b. Zechariah 7: 12
7. What underlying attitudes cause you to disregard godly counsel?

　　　a. Deuteronomy 1: 43

　　　b. 2 Kings 17: 14-15

　　　c. Psalm 81: 11-12

　　　d. Ezekiel 3: 7

8. What happens when godly counsel is followed?

　　　a. Psalm 73:24

　　　b. Proverbs 24:3-6

　　　c. Jeremiah 26: 3

　　　d. Luke 6: 46-48

9. What attitude should be used when giving advice?

　　　a. Proverbs 15: 1

　　　b. Ecclesiastes 12: 9-10

Trust God to Make the Move

It took Ilyssa a while to settle down from Marissa's rude and manipulative comments. But after a long Bible study session and a lot of prayer, God settled her mind and she was able to think with less emotional outrage. Ilyssa had to admit Marissa had made a few good points. "Maybe we should check out this new job offer a little more thoroughly and ask God which part of your mom's message he wants us to hear," Ilyssa suggested to Leo later that night.

Try This:

Reflect on God's word about giving and receiving advice and opinions. Prayerfully finish these sentences.

1. Before giving my advice or opinion, I will ...

2. When I give advice, my tone will be ...

3. Next time my in-law gives me her advice or opinion, I will ...

An Ending Thought

"The moment we begin to fear the opinions of others and hesitate to tell the truth that is in us, and, from motives of policy, are silent when we should speak, the divine floods of light and life no longer flow into our souls."

　　　　　　　　　　　　–Women's suffragist, Elizabeth Cady Stanton

All the quotes below are from mothers and daughters-in-law who describe their relationship as above average.

DAUGHTER-IN-LAW QUOTE:

The best thing I can say about my in-law is "she is a very godly woman who would do anything for me."

I show affection to my in-law by "telling her I love her, calling her frequently, and spending quality time with her."

MOTHER-IN-LAW QUOTES:

I show affection to my in-law by "doing things that will relieve her stress, hugging her, and talking to her on the phone."

I show affection to my in-law by "offering to baby-sit so she and my son can have a date night alone."

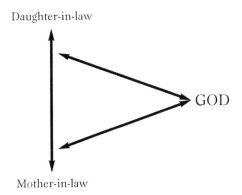

※ ※ ※

Loving Lora

D*ear friend, let us love one another, for love comes from God* (1John 4:7a, New International Version).

Mother-in-law's Side

When my stepson Bill married Lisa, my husband Walter and I were skeptical. Her character was so different from the type of woman we would have chosen for him. Lisa was very smart and pretty, but extremely independent, opinionated, domineering, and strong-willed. Her upbringing was totally different from Bill's; he was a southerner and she was raised on the north-east coast. She came from a non-religious background and was definitely career-oriented.

To make the gap between us bigger, Bill's mother, Walter's ex-wife, began telling Lisa untrue stories about Walter and me. As a step-mother-to-be, I knew I would have to work very hard to develop a good relationship with these two young people. Bill's mother's continual criticism of me had created skepticism in their hearts. It was hard for them not to believe her untrue reports. This made the space between Lisa and I seem almost like the Grand Canyon.

Bill and Lisa's wedding was beautiful, but Walter and I felt totally left out. I wondered how we would ever have a meaningful relationship with Bill and Lisa. As time passed, our visits and communication were infrequent, and I felt we were doomed to a long-distance relationship without any depth. However, within five years, God blessed us with a beautiful granddaughter and adorable twin grandsons. Our relationship with Bill and Lisa began to slowly warm as we adored these precious grandchildren and appreciated the effort it took to love and nurture them. Walter and I praised Bill and Lisa for the great job they were doing caring for their children.

But soon after the twins were born, Lisa was diagnosed with a life-threatening disease. To make matters worse, just prior to Lisa's diagnosis, Bill had accepted a new job in another town. Their home had sold quickly, and they only had a few days to move out. So Walter and I quickly caught a plane to be at Bill and Lisa's side to help in any way we could. We spent several days packing their belongings, caring for the children, and helping Bill settle into an apartment where he and the children would live temporarily while Lisa was receiving the medical care she needed. Thankfully Bill's new company allowed him all the time he needed to be at Lisa's side.

News of Lisa's illness was shocking, and the time getting through her hospitalization was difficult; but somehow we managed to pack the house, help care for the children, and offer support to Bill and Lisa. We know it was only with the Lord's help that we had the opportunity and strength to do this.

Amazingly, just prior to that difficult time, friends had invited Bill and Lisa to a Bible-believing church. As they attended church, God's word began to take root in their hearts and minds. During Lisa's hospitalization and following, the church family supported them with prayers and love, and faith began to grow in Bill and Lisa's life.

Something wonderful also began to happen to our relationship with Bill and Lisa during those dark days. Lisa noticed how we immediately came to be with her family during their crisis to help and support in anyway we could. And she began to understand our intentions were genuine and that we really wanted a loving relationship with her and Bill. It didn't take her long to realize the unkind things Bill's mother had said about us weren't true. She began to recognize we really did trust God and loved being a part of her family.

Since before their marriage, Walter and I had been asking God to help us develop a meaningful relationship with Bill and Lisa. He was faithful to answer that prayer, even though it was certainly not in the way we would have chosen. Within months after her ordeal, Lisa began gaining strength, and we praise God for His care of her. Each of us learned a lot during this time. The crisis especially taught us never to take God's blessings for granted, to continue trusting Him, and to persevere in prayer.

Daughter-in-law's Side

I had been raised to believe that Christianity was for gullible people, and those who claimed to be Christians were either frauds, whose main objective was to mislead others for their own financial gain, or who were so simple-minded, they had managed to be deceived themselves. Church seemed to be an archaic structure that continued to survive for the exploitation of weak people. The Bible, I believed – though I had never read it, was a book filled with fantasy and myth. I could not fathom the idea of what Christian love meant much less that it actually existed.

During our engagement and following our marriage, Bill's mother added validity to my misguided beliefs about Christianity. She told me a lot of things about Lora, Bill's stepmother, that sadly I believed and that colored my opinion of Lora and Walter. She had convinced me that they were religious fanatics and that I should steer clear of them. Though they seemed really thrilled when our children were born, keeping distance from them really wasn't a problem since they lived several states away and rarely interfered in our relationship.

Our relationship would have probably continued on like that, but not long after the birth of the twins, I was diagnosed with an advanced stage of breast cancer. This diagnosis meant leaving my young children with my parents who were ridden with their own health issues while Bill stayed with me in the hospital. Lora and Walter flew out the next day to help in anyway they could.

I probably would have been skeptical of their intentions, but Bill and I had recently been introduced to Jesus Christ. Prior to my cancer, some of my friends had invited us to a Bible-based church. Though cynical, we started attending and, for the first time, really began to hear the Bible preached and began to understand what its message and Christ's birth, death, and resurrection meant for our personal lives. During my hospitalization, the church came to our side just as Walter and Lora had, and I began to see Walter and Lora in a different light. And as my trust in Jesus Christ grew, I began to see we had more in common with Bill's dad and step-mom than I had previously believed. They prayed with me and pitched in to help anyway they could. Their actions showed me they were sincere, and their faith was real. Walter and Lora stayed long enough to help us settle into an apartment and care for the children. As months passed, Lora flew back and forth to help while I was in and out of the hospital. During my illness, they were both loving and helpful.

I thank God I am in remission now and able to care for our children once again. I am also very grateful I now have a warm relationship with Walter and Lora, who continue to encourage us and provide a Christ-like example for us. But, most of all, I thank God that Bill and I are now firm believers in Jesus Christ.

God's Angle- Love

Actions speak louder than words. This old saying was true in Lisa's case. Lora's unconditional love came through as real and genuine. God's words lived out were powerful in reflecting the love of God. This is the same love Jesus Christ lived out when he gave His life that we might have eternal life. He redirected His will for the benefit of the world when He said to His Father God about His upcoming crucifixion, *"yet not my will but yours be done"* (Luke 22:42, New International Version). Jesus willingly went to the cross as God's only provision for your sins. It is through Him that you can know and experience this love (Romans 5: 8). As you redirect your will for the benefit of others, it reflects your true love for them. Indeed, it is Christ's love in you that is reflected in you to others. It is hard to continually reject God's love in another person.

The Bible reveals much about God's love. It

- is unfailing- Psalm 51: 1, 52: 8, 90: 14
- endures- 2 Chronicles 5: 13, 7: 3, 20: 21
- abounds - Psalm 86: 5

According to The Apostle Paul in 1 Corinthians 13, you can possess spiritual gifts but, if you do not have love, you are nothing. Then He reminds you what love is.

1. Love is patient.
2. Love is kind.
3. Love does not envy.
4. Love does not boast.
5. Love is not rude.
6. Love is not self-seeking.
7. Love is not easily angered.
8. Love keeps no record of wrong.
9. Love does not delight in wrong.
10. Love rejoices with the truth.
11. Love always protects.
12. Love always trusts.
13. Love always hopes.
14. Love always perseveres.
15. Love never fails.

1 John 4: 14, 16-19 says of love; you can know that you live in God and that He lives in you because He has given you His Spirit. It is a Spirit of love since God is love. And so if you live in love, you live in God and God lives in you. In this way, love is made complete in and through you so you will have confidence on Judgment Day. You will have confidence because in this world you are becoming more like Jesus. Fear will not cripple you because Christ's perfect love that lives in you drives out fear. He loved you first, and so now you love.

Where Are You on The Triangle?
Reflect on your relationship with your in-law and honestly answer
the following.

1. Have you come to know Jesus Christ as your personal Lord
    and Savior? If so, what changes have taken place in your life?
    How are these changes reflected in your in-law relationship?
2. Would you say you live a blameless life (Psalm 101:2) or are
    you in need of forgiveness?
3. Do you seek to follow Jesus in all your ways – even in your in-
    law relationship?
4. Do you keep records of ways your in-law has wronged you?
5. Are you willing to pray and ask God to help you love your in-
    law as He loves you (John 15:12)?

Finding God's Perspective
Use a Bible to help you answer the question below.
Put yourself in your in-law's shoes. As you read each verse think,
"How would my in-law see me through this scripture?"

1. Proverb 10: 12 (love covers all wrongs)
2. Matthew 5: 44 (love your enemies)
3. Luke 6: 32-36 (then your reward will be great)
4. Romans 12: 9-10 (cling to what is good)

Trust God to Make the Move
God showed Lisa that Lora's love for the Lord and for her was
greater than Lora's love for herself. Are you willing to trust God's will
and accept His good pleasure in your relationship with your in-law
(Philippians 2:13)?
Try This:

1. Read 1John 4:7-12. Think about your in-law. Write a prayer
    to the Lord.
2. After you have written the Lord a prayer, ask God to help you
    write one to yourself from Him. Is God asking you to change

an attitude toward your in-law?

An Ending Thought

"What lies behind us and what lies before us are tiny matters compared to what lies within us."

–Ralph Waldo Emerson

About the Authors

Pam Eason   Jane Jones   Jane Mills

The authors, mothers and daughters-in-law all, share a love for Jesus Christ and a love for family. All are published authors, conference speakers, Bible-study teachers, and former educators who met at Community Bible Study in Destin, Florida where Jane Mills and Pam Eason still reside.

Jane Jones, author of *From Grief to Gladness-Coming Back from Widowhood*, is the mother of three children and has four grandchildren and one great-grandchild. She now lives in Knoxville, Tennessee. Jane Mills is the mother of two sons and has ten grandchildren. Pam Eason is the mother of a son and a daughter and has two grandchildren.

To contact the authors, email:

Pam Eason at myhonestanswers@gmail.com

Jane Jones at jgjcove@tds.net

Jane Mills at jm267@cox.net

Printed in the United States
69245LVS00001B/208-798